# THINGS YOU NEED TO

## Pen Keyte

Oxford University Press

Oxford University Press, Walton Street, Oxford OX2 6DP

Oxford New York Toronto
Delhi Bombay Calcutta Madras Karachi
Petaling Jaya Singapore Hong Kong Tokyo
Nairobi Dar es Salaam Cape Town
Melbourne Auckland

and associated companies in
Beirut Berlin Ibadan Nicosia

*Oxford* is a trade mark of Oxford University Press

## Acknowledgements

The Publishers would like to thank the following for permission to reproduce photographic
material:
Philip Atkins: p. 36 (top left); Advertising Standards Authority: p. 71; Banking Information
Service: p. 87 (top); Barclays Bank: pp. 86 (top), 89 (right); British Rail: pp. 27, 69; British
Telecom: p. 49; Tom Butler, Family Planning Association: p. 140; Cadbury Ltd: p. 69; Careers
and Occupational Information Centre: p. 95; Careers Office, Oxford: p. 100; J. Allan Cash Ltd:
p. 36 (top right); Coca Cola: p. 69; Eggs Authority: p. 69; Geographers' A–Z Map Company Ltd:
p. 31; Job Centre, Oxford: p. 101; The Joint Credit Card Company Ltd: p. 89; King's Arms,
Oxford: p. 149; Marks and Spencer plc: p. 62; Ordnance Survey: p. 31; *The Oxford Journal*:
p. 130; Rosie Potter: pp. 145 (inset), 154; Top of the Pops, BBC: p. 65; UB40 Drop-in Centre,
Oxford: p. 114; Voluntary Service Bureau, Oxford: p. 111; Charlotte Ward-Perkins: pp. 101, 154
(bottom); *Which?*: p. 127; Terry Williams: p. 145 (main picture).

All other photos are by Chris Honeywell.

The illustrations are by Patricia Capon, Ian Heard, Peter Joyce, Viv Mabon and Nigel Paige.

Cover illustration: Sue Heap

The author gratefully acknowledges the help provided by the following: Belmores, Family
Planning Association, Oxfordshire Health Education Unit, Community Health Council for
Oxfordshire, Medical Defence Union, Trades Union Congress.

The information in this book is correct at the time of writing, but some of the facts may become
outdated. Up-to-date information can be obtained from the organizations listed in the Useful
Addresses section at the back of this book.

Typeset by Oxford Publishing Services, Oxford
Printed and bound in Great Britain by William Clowes Limited, Beccles and London

# Contents

# Introduction for the teacher

Recent innovations in examination syllabuses bring with them a change in teaching focus, away from subject-centred, entirely classroom-based teaching and learning, to a more pupil-centred approach, which seeks to equip young people with information which will be of use to them in their adult life.

One way of helping people to gain control over their lives is to give them the information which they need. A better way is to help them develop the skills and confidence to find things out for themselves, and to make use of what they find. This book sets out to do two things: to provide information which young people need, and to suggest activities and exercises which put that information into use.

The following symbols are used:

indicates factual resource material

indicates discussion questions

indicates that a written response is needed

indicates role play

indicates that students must research or survey a topic themselves

indicates that students should interview other people on the subject

indicates that students should think up and practise saying the appropriate questions or statements.

Skills and confidence can only be acquired through practice. Pieces of reference or factual material are therefore only infrequently followed by written exercises designed to test what students have learnt. Exercises more often ask people to discuss, to practise saying things or asking questions, to role play, to interview others, to decide for themselves on the best course of action, to find things out for themselves, and to develop work themselves, which may take them outside the classroom.

As a teacher, you may already be using these methods. For those to whom such ideas are new, here are some guidelines and suggestions which may prove useful.

# Classroom organization

Depending on the size of your group, the existing classroom arrangement may not be suitable. For example, it isn't easy to have a discussion if people are sitting in rows and can't see each other. You may have to rearrange furniture. Small groups are best for a number of these activities. If you have to divide up a large group, make sure that each smaller group appoints a leader and/or secretary to report back at the end, so that each group can compare findings.

# The role of the teacher

In life skills, the teacher is only 'expert' insofar as he or she has experienced more and reflected further than the students. But the experiences and reflections of the students are no less valid than the teacher's. Both teacher and students frequently have difficulty in coming to terms with a situation in which the teacher is not saying precisely what should happen or be done. In particular, students may be reluctant to take on the organization of their own learning. Ideally, the life skills teacher is an enabler, who sets up conditions which the students then take over and run for themselves. It is reasonable for students to expect teachers to participate in discussions and to contribute from their own experience. Both teacher and student can refuse to answer questions which they feel to be too personal.

# Other resources

It is hoped that, where possible, teachers will exploit local conditions and resources, by introducing outside speakers, arranging visits, and developing their own exercises. If they are available, cassette recorders and video recorders help in evaluating what learning has taken place.

# Running the exercises

Most of the exercises need an introduction, explaining what the group as a whole is going to set out to do. Role plays and simulations should only be tried when the group has warmed up, and only with a group whose members know each other, and the teacher, well.

It is the teacher's responsibility to be aware of role-playing situations which are particularly sensitive for his or her students. At the end of the role-play, it is most important to allow time and opportunity for students to come out of their roles. Allow time at the end of the lesson therefore, for students to replay the exercise with changed roles, and/or to talk about what has gone on. If the teacher is not directly involved in the role play, he or she can observe what is going on, and devise appropriate questions so that students can evaluate the exercise.

Finally, the suggested exercises are only ideas; they are to be abandoned, extended, and developed as you think fit.

# 1 Living

This chapter is about what people do when they are not at school or work. It covers:
- relationships with the family
- leaving home and finding somewhere to live
- organizing leisure time
- the environment.

Some of the facts come from recent reports and research work. Writers make statements about what the *majority* of people do; what they say may not apply to you. If you disagree with what they say, say so!

## The family

### Some facts about young people and their families

Most young people are greatly influenced by their families. They tend to share the family's attitudes and values. Up to the age of about 14, most young people spend most of their leisure time with their families. After this age, young people begin to break away from the family and to become more independent. Generally, families approve of this; they are interested in what their children do, and continue to support them in their developing independence.

## Recent changes in the family

The typical family used to be thought of as two parents and two children living in the same house. Today, only 15% of families fit this model. Young people are now more likely to live with only one parent, and to have one step-parent and step-brothers and sisters.

One in three marriages today will probably end in divorce. Over the last twenty years, divorce has increased by 500%. Teenage marriages are particularly at risk. If a girl marries in her teens, her marriage is twice as likely to end in divorce as that of a girl marrying aged 20–24, and four times as likely to end in divorce as that of a girl marrying aged 25–29.

One in five children born today will have parents who divorce before the children are 16 years old.

## Household types

Here is a table of the different types of household in Britain. Have a look at it and answer the questions that follow. A 'dependent' child is one who needs to be looked after by the family. An 'independent' child can look after him or herself, and so is probably earning or has left home.

**Households: by type** Great Britain

|  | 1961 % | 1980 % |
|---|---|---|
| *One person* | | |
| — under retirement age | 4 | 8 |
| — over retirement age | 7 | 14 |
| *Two or more people* | | |
| — one or more over retirement age | 3 | 1 |
| — all under retirement age | 2 | 1 |
| *Family* | | |
| Married couple only | 26 | 27 |
| Married couple with 1 or 2 dependent children | 30 | 26 |
| Married couple with 3 or more dependent children | 8 | 6 |
| Married couple with independent child(ren) only | 10 | 8 |
| Lone parent with at least one dependent child | 2 | 4 |
| Lone parent with independent child(ren) only | 4 | 4 |
| *Two or more families* | 3 | 1 |
| *Total households* | 100 | 100 |

Source: *Social Trends*, 12, HMSO, 1981, Table 2.2.

1 Has the number of one-person households gone up or down? Why do you think this is?
2 Has the number of married couples with dependent children gone up or down? Why do you think this is?
3 Has the number of one-parent families with dependent children gone up or down? Why do you think this is?

Look at this table which shows the different types of one-parent families:

**Different types of one-parent families**, Great Britain, 1979

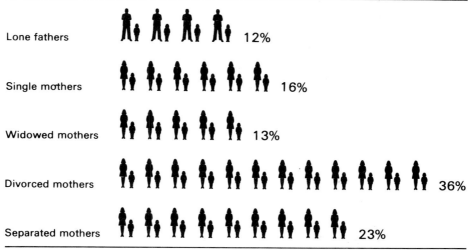

| | |
|---|---|
| Lone fathers | 12% |
| Single mothers | 16% |
| Widowed mothers | 13% |
| Divorced mothers | 36% |
| Separated mothers | 23% |

Source: House of Commons *Hansard*, HMSO, 23 July 1981

Add up the total percentage of women bringing up children on their own. How much is it? Is it greater or smaller than the number of men bringing up children on their own? Can you suggest why this is?

In spite of these figures, the family unit still remains the most important social institution in our society. Most young people will marry. An increasing number of them will live with their partners before marriage.

## The family and work

This table shows how the labour force was made up in this country in 1921 and 1979:

**The composition of the labour force**, Great Britain

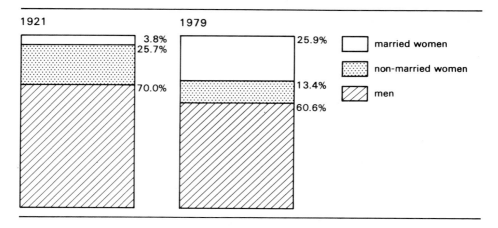

1921
3.8%
25.7%
70.0%

1979
25.9%
13.4%
60.6%

married women

non-married women

men

Two more facts:
- Young people enter the labour market at a later age than they used to.
- The number of older men and women in work is going down.

**?**

1 What reasons can you give for the two statements above?
2 Why are mothers less likely to work than women without children?
3 Why are they more likely to do part-time work?
4 What contribution do you think the mother makes to the family income?
5 What are the disadvantages for the mother and her family of her going out to work?
6 What are the advantages?
7 Has the number of married women in work gone up or down since 1921? Why do you think this is?

The majority of fathers work full time, and those with large families tend to work longer hours than fathers with small families. Fathers of young children are more likely to do overtime and work shifts.

1 Why do you think this is?
2 What effect do you think it might have on the family?

### The elderly

People now tend to live longer. Elderly people often find it increasingly difficult to look after themselves. It is usually the family, not Social Services, that provides the necessary care.

**?**

1 What effect do you think looking after an elderly relative would have on the family?
2 Which members of the family are most likely to do the actual caring?
3 What would this caring involve?

## Living at home

**»**

Do a survey in your class to find out the number of people who live with:
a one parent
b both parents
c more than one brother or sister
d dependent elderly relatives
e other people or relatives in the home — e.g. sister's fiancé.

## What do you and your friends think about living at home?

➡ Read these statements and rate them out of 6. 6 means they are very true for you; 0 means that they are not at all true for you.

1 I am happy at home and don't think I'll leave.
2 I want to leave home now.
3 I don't want to leave home yet but I will when I'm 18 or so.
4 Things are getting worse at home. It used to be all right.
5 Things at home are better now I'm older.
6 My mum/dad is always going on at me.
7 My dad/mum and I don't get on.
8 My brother/sister gets treated differently.
9 My parents are strict but I don't mind.
10 My parents are strict and it gets on my nerves.
11 I'm scared about living on my own.
12 I think I'm expected to do too much in the house.
13 I won't leave home till I'm married.
14 When I'm married I think it would be nice to live with my mum and dad.

If you feel that things aren't going as well at home as they used to, try doing the rest of this section. It looks at the reasons why some people of your age suddenly find home life difficult, and what you can do to make it better.

➡ First, let's look at your life at home a couple of years ago. Can you finish this statement?

Compared with a couple of years ago, life at home now is . . .

What things have brought about the change? Have some members of the family left, have new members arrived?

➡ Finish these sentences:
I hate it when my mum or dad…
I like it when they…
I feel happy when they…

❓ What sorts of things cause rows between you and your parents at home? What would your mum or dad say in these situations?

1 They've found you smoking.

2 You want to go to an all-night party with a friend of the same sex.
3 You want to go to an all-night party with a friend of the opposite sex.
4 You say you don't want to visit your grandparents any more.

5 You'd like more pocket money.
6 You want to choose more of your clothes yourself.
7 You want to be paid for jobs you do in the house.
8 You want your girl/boyfriend to stay the night.
9 You want to stay with your girl/boyfriend.
10 You want to decorate your bedroom.
11 You want a Saturday job.
12 You've decided not to do your homework.
13 You don't want to go on the family holiday this year.
14 You have a new friend of whom your parents don't approve.

*If you're a boy:* Do you think your parents' reactions might be different if you were a girl? If so, why?
*If you're a girl:* Do you think your parents' reactions might be different if you were a boy? If so, why?

Choose four of the above situations, and role-play them with someone else. You should play a parent, your partner should play you. You say what you think your parent would say.

Can you say what seems to be your mum or dad's favourite expression when talking to you?

## Your parents' expectations

Most parents have hopes and perhaps even ambitions for their children.

What words would you use to describe these sort of remarks? Which of the following?

helpful                     puzzled
hurtful                     feeling hurt
critical                    feeling left out
lacking in understanding

Are there any other words you would use to describe them?
How do you think the parents in these pictures feel?

12

Perhaps your parents aren't intending to be hurtful or critical; they just want the best for you. Can you think of recent examples where you've been hurt by something your parents said, which might have been said because they were trying to help?

### Talking to parents

Who would you go to if you felt you were in trouble? Would you go to your parents:

definitely
probably
perhaps
probably not
definitely not
it would depend what the problem was?

Can you say when you think your parents realized that you occasionally took more notice of what other people said than what they said?
When were the occasions? Do they occur more frequently now?
Maybe one of the results of this is that your parents feel a bit left out of your life; there are bound to be things that you feel are private and don't want to talk to them about.

The more she says those awful things, the less I want to talk to her.
Anyway, he's not a boyfriend, and we just talk about this and that. Nothing much. Why must she pry?

You never tell me about your friends / boyfriends / what you do in your room / what you talk about. I think you're trying to keep it a secret from me.

Do you think the mother is prying?
Do you think the teenager is secretive?
How could they keep talking to each other?
What could the teenager say to her mother to explain?
What could she ask her mother about her own teenage years that would help the mother remember what it was like?

Role-play some of the things that have been said, and how you would react.

### Changes in your parents' lives

Your parents are probably pleased to see you growing more independent, but it might seem to them to be happening very quickly. The days when you were almost entirely dependent on them for everything, and when you turned to them for advice and protection, seem only a short time away. They may not quite have made the adjustment. Have you heard them say things like this, which seem like contradictions?

It's time you did that for yourself.

Oh let me do that for you, you only make a mess.

It's time you made up your own mind.

You never do a thing I say.

Think of some more yourself.

Can you think of other things, apart from their children growing up, which are changing in your parents' lives?
Any of the following?

> Your father is worried about redundancy.
> Your father has lost his job.
> Your father is having to work more overtime to keep his income up.
> Your mother has gone back to work full time.
> Your mother says she wants to go back to work.
> Your parents' marriage isn't working well.
> Your parents are worried about your elder brothers or sisters.
> There's a new baby in the family.

## The home

How much work is there in running a home? Make a list of all the jobs that you can think of. Compare your list with other people's.
Beside each job, write the following:
- how often it has to be done
- who does it
- what help you give
- whether the job has to be done partly or entirely because you are there.

Look at the list, and complete the sentence below:
When I looked at my list, I was surprised to see that...

When Vincent did this exercise, he was surprised to see that there were some jobs that he'd never realized had to be done, and also that he didn't know who did them — but it certainly wasn't him!

I began to realize what a lot of work there was to be done in a home, and also, since my mum is a single mum and goes out to work, what a lot she had to do. Perhaps that's why she's always tired and not always good to be with.

What jobs do you think Vincent could help with in the home?

Unless you're desperately unhappy — in which case, you ought to talk to someone about it — home is the best place to stay if you:
- are still at school
- are going to a local college, training course, or YTS programme
- leave school without a job and go on the dole
- are employed on a low wage near home.

This is because finding somewhere to live is difficult and expensive. You definitely shouldn't think of leaving home if you have nowhere to go.

### Your contribution

Once you have left school and are earning or drawing Social Security, or have a training allowance, you and your parents may decide it's time you contributed to the family budget. You may do this already, of course, especially if you have a part-time job.

**?** What do you think is a reasonable contribution for a sixteen-year-old to make in the following circumstances?
1 In a full-time job with take-home pay of £45 per week.
2 On a training course with an allowance of £30 per week.
3 On supplementary benefit.
4 In a part-time job bringing home £15 a week.
5 In undeclared work where the earnings are very different from week to week.

# Leaving home

At sixteen, you can leave home with your parents' consent. If they do agree to your going, it might be a good idea to take them with you to look at places you think might suit you. Your parents will be able to advise you on whether the place is right for you. You may well overlook things like damp or lack of heating, which they will notice. It also impresses landlords and landladies if they can see you've got your parents' approval.

If you are desperately unhappy at home, and even thinking of leaving without your parents' consent, you should talk to someone first. You could try a youth worker, or refer yourself to Social Services. They will expect you to tell them what your problems are.

Before you leave home, you need to know where you're going. Single housing is usually difficult to find, and expensive. It can be difficult to claim Social Security benefits without an address.

**?** What do you think would be a good reason for leaving home, and what would be a bad reason? What about these reasons?
1 Your aunt has offered you a place in her house because there are better job prospects where she lives.
2 Your best friend who has gone to college has said you can sleep on his or her floor.
3 Accommodation is provided while you're being trained.

**4** You get a live-in job and you're fairly sure you can get on with the people.

**5** You and your boy/girlfriend want to set up home together.

**6** You think you'll go to the nearest big town to look for work, though you haven't got anywhere to live there.

**7** You're on the dole.

Once you've decided that leaving home is the right thing for you, there are a lot of things you need to know or to find out:
- the types of accommodation available
- which one suits you best
- how to find it
- whether you can afford it
- how to survive on your own.

These questions are dealt with next.


# On your own

Look at these young people's experiences. Which of their problems are to do with:
- having to share with other people?
- being inexperienced themselves?
- not having a lot of money?
- not being very good at managing money?

Some of these places, they ask you for a large deposit and a month's rent in advance. That's a lot of money to find.

The people upstairs are always having all-night parties.

The first time I cooked a meal in my new place, I spent all the week's food allowance on a joint of meat. Never again.

I'd never thought about the problem of drying washing. You haul it back from the laundrette, and once I hadn't dried it properly. I left these things in a plastic bag and they went mouldy.

When I moved out, the landlord kept the deposit, because he said I'd damaged the furniture. It was like that when I moved in, but I couldn't prove it.

# Types of accommodation available

### Live-in accommodation

**?** Live-in accommodation comes with certain jobs. Do you know what sort of jobs might provide you with a room and meals as well?
Why do you think accommodation is provided?
Which of these jobs might provide accommodation:

> caretaker, forester, engineer, baker, janitor, forecourt attendant, maintenance worker, nanny, childminder, shop assistant, tyre fitter, mother's help, gardener, au pair, farm labourer, hotel work, painter and decorator, armed forces, secretary, hairdresser?

Which of these jobs are suitable for young people?
Which would not be suitable for young people? Why not?
Do you think that workers who live in, and maybe receive meals as well, earn a high or low wage? Why?
What would be the disadvantages of working as a live-in mother's help or as a live-in gardener?

### Lodgings

ROOM TO LET IN PLEASANT FAMILY. SUIT SINGLE PROFESSIONAL PERSON. BREAKFAST AND EVENING MEAL, NO EXTRAS.

ROOM TO LET. WOULD SUIT FOREIGN STUDENT.

Room for female willing to help elderly lady with light domestic duties.

VACANT ROOM. SUIT SINGLE WORKING MAN IN HIS TWENTIES.

**?** You can see that some landlords prefer certain types of lodger.
Why do you think they might prefer:

> foreign students
> females
> people in their twenties
> single professional people
> working people?

'Lodging' means staying in someone's house, usually with the owner on the premises. You pay for a room, which you may have to share, and some meals are provided. Your washing may be done for you. The cost is quite high — maybe as much as £45 per week in some parts of the country — but you don't have to pay extra for electricity, gas, and so on. You're still living with a family.

**?** Why might this be a good thing?
How might it be different from living at home?
In what ways do you think it would be better?
In what ways do you think it might be worse?
What might the problems be about:

| | |
|---|---|
| food | freedom to come and go |
| noise | using things like the phone or kitchen |
| having visitors | privacy? |

Because you are living in the landlord's house and he is providing some services, you are not a protected tenant (see p. 20). He can therefore ask you to leave at very short notice. You don't usually sign any agreement with him.

▶ Make a list of the advantages and disadvantages of lodgings. What sort of person would this accommodation suit?

## Renting a bedsit

A bedsit is one room, in which you sleep, eat, live, and perhaps cook as well. There may be something like a gas ring or a small cooker (two plates and a grill) in your room. Or you may instead share a kitchen with other people in the house. You'll almost certainly share a toilet and bathroom. Bedsits are usually in large houses, so there may be a lot of other people, whom you don't know, in the house.

? What equipment would you expect to find in a bedsit?
What might you have to provide for yourself?

**Advantages:**
It's a good start to an independent life, if you can cope on your own.
You're responsible only for the electricity and gas you yourself use — it'll probably be metered. So you don't have to worry about rows over bills with other tenants.

**Disadvantages:**
It can be lonely. Having a lot of people living in the same house may not prevent this. You and they may not get on.
You may have to pay a deposit and/or rent in advance.

? Things to decide for yourself about living in a bedsit:
       What things would I find it difficult to cope with in a bedsit?
       What sort of neighbours would I find it hard to get on with?
       Would I mind being in a house with people I don't know?
       Would I mind sharing toilet, bathroom, and maybe kitchen?
       Can I manage to look after myself?
       How easy would I find it to get enough cash together for the deposit and rent in advance?
       Do I mind if the place is badly decorated and furnished?

## Renting a flat

Renting a flat is expensive, so you'll probably share the flat. You have a bedroom, which may be shared. You share the kitchen and bathroom with the other people in your flat.

Because landlords like only one name on the lease, one of you has to sign the lease and is therefore legally obliged to pay, whether or not the others have paid him or her.

### Advantages:

It can be pleasant and work out well if you get on with the people you share with, and can sort out bills between you.

### Disadvantages:

You may find that you don't get on with the people you're sharing with.
Some people may not do their share of the communal jobs such as cleaning.
You may have difficulty deciding how to share out the bills.
The flat itself may be damp, poorly equipped, or badly furnished.

Here are some comments from people who have shared flats:

The independence and freedom was great.

It all worked well the first few months. We had this communal system for buying food and paying bills.

But some people had more money than others, and in the end we abandoned the system because not everyone could afford it.

I got fed up with always buying the milk and cleaning the bath.

We first looked at the place in the summer, and it looked very nice. I never thought about what it would be like in the winter. Because it's a basement it's very cold, damp and dark. We had to spend a lot on electricity.

I think it really made me grow up, having to look after myself. And I made some good friends thanks to the other people in the flat.

From some of the comments made above, write or draw a story about what you think it's like to share a flat. Put in some of the good things, and some of the bad things. What do you think people can do about the bad things?

## Money

The cost of renting a flat varies from place to place, and is usually most expensive in big cities. From the column of your local newspaper, find out what the going rate for shared flats is in your area. What do these abbreviations mean?

Per w.   Pcm.   incl.   excl.   Mod cons.
sh. rm.   Own rm.   mxd hse.   O/r.

From the advertisements in your local paper, answer these questions:
1  Do any specify whether male or female is preferred?
2  What is the price range of rented accommodation? What do you seem to get for the most expensive?
3  How many are shared rooms?
4  Do any specify 'prof. person reqd'? What does the 'prof.' mean?
5  If you were offered one of the rooms and had to pay a deposit of one month's rent, plus one month's rent in advance, how much would that come to? Can you estimate how many weeks' wages it represents for a young person in his/her first job?

## Tenants' rights

If you rent a room or flat, you are a *tenant*. You have some legal rights, but the area is confusing, because there are different categories of tenant. Before you sign anything or commit yourself to renting, get advice on the terms of your lease. Go to the Citizens' Advice Bureau, or a Housing Aid Centre, or a Law Centre.

One important thing to discover is whether you are a protected tenant or an unprotected tenant. If you are a protected tenant, you have certain rights. You cannot be made to leave unless the landlord can give good reasons which will stand up in a court of law.

### Protected tenants

- live in furnished or unfurnished accommodation where the landlord does not live in the same house, *or*
- have inherited the protected tenancy from a relative who has died, provided that they have lived with the relative for six months before the death.

The landlord has the right to ask protected tenants to leave if:
- they have not paid rent or gas and electricity bills
- they have damaged the property
- they have been a nuisance to other tenants
- they have broken the tenancy agreement through subletting or using the premises for illegal or immoral purposes
- the landlord wants the property for himself or his family to live in.

Tenants have less protection if they:
- live in furnished or unfurnished accommodation where the landlord shares the accommodation, or lives in part of the house
- live in accommodation where the landlord provides them with meals
- take a fixed-term or holiday let, where they agree with the landlord to leave on a certain date
- pay very low annual rents, that is less than two-thirds of the rateable value of the property (for an explanation of what rateable value is, see page 119)
- live in accommodation which is rented from an institution, for example, students in a hall of residence.

## Other things to look out for if you are renting accommodation

### Getting organized

Places go very quickly. If you are phoning up and making appointments to view several places, you will need to keep a note of the names and addresses of landlords that you are contacting. You'll need enough money to phone them all. You'll need to know how to get there.

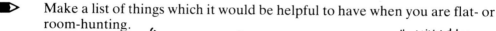

Make a list of things which it would be helpful to have when you are flat- or room-hunting.

### Meeting the landlord

What sort of questions may he or she want to ask you? What questions can you ask him or her? How can you make a good impression?
- If you have to give a deposit, ask for a receipt.
- If you are a weekly tenant, make sure you get a rent book, which will record the date and amount of rent paid.

### Contracts

A contract, agreement, or lease sets out the arrangements made between you (the tenant) and the landlord. It must state:
- the amount of rent to be paid
- whether the rent is paid weekly or monthly
- how much rent you must pay in advance

- when the rent is due
- how much notice the landlord must give before he can raise the rent
- how much notice each of you must give before ending the contract
- the length of time the agreement is to run
- any special rules or conditions about subletting, pets, and so on.

Read the contract before you sign it. If there is something you don't understand, ask for advice first from the Citizens' Advice Bureau or a Law Centre or a Housing Aid Centre.

### The inventory

This is a list of things which the landlord has provided in the flat. Read it first, check that things are there, and then sign it. Otherwise you may have signed for things that aren't there. Point out any furniture that looks torn or broken, so that you don't get blamed for it. But if you do break or lose anything, the landlord can charge you for it, and take it out of the deposit.

I didn't pay much attention to the inventory, but when the time came for me to leave, the landlord kept most of my deposit because he said I'd broken things and damaged the furniture. It wasn't true, but I couldn't prove it.

**?** Tenants can't be held responsible for damage which is done as a result of 'fair wear and tear'; some things do wear out eventually. What damage do you think counts as 'fair wear and tear'?

### Council housing

Local authorities must by law give aid to all homeless people and people threatened with homelessness who come to them for help. At the moment, local authorities provide homes for about a third of all householders in Britain. But there is a waiting list in most parts of Britain, because there is not enough council housing to meet the demand. Local authorities have a system of giving priority to people with the most need. Preference is given to:
- people who have lived in the area for a certain period of time
- people with families
- people made homeless by fire and flood
- the disabled and elderly.

The priority groups do not include single people, except in special circumstances such as:
- old age
- mental illness or handicap
- being pregnant or having young children
- being disabled.

The vast majority of young single people do not therefore usually have access to council housing. But some local authorities offer special schemes for young people, usually in accommodation which is unsuitable for families.

➤➤ Find out whether your local authority provides any special schemes for housing young people.

❓ Many people have special needs. How would you allocate priorities to the homeless?

### The dangers of homelessness

It's a very bad idea to leave home with no place to go at all. The situation gets worse because:

- you may spend all your money very quickly on bed and breakfasts or hostels
- it's very difficult to get a job without somewhere to live
- if you start sleeping rough you won't be able to look after yourself properly and won't look presentable for job interviews
- although you can claim supplementary benefit without an address, you will get less than if you have somewhere to live.

# Leisure

❓ What is leisure, and who has it? Look at this list of people and what they are doing. Which of them do you think are 'working', and which of them are occupied in a leisure pursuit?

> a mother of two young children who stays at home to look after them
> an unemployed teenager who is looking for work
> a retired couple doing their garden
> a painter/decorator when he is doing up his own house at weekends
> a voluntary helper at the local Family Planning Clinic
> a nurse making silver jewelry at weekends and selling it.

If a hobby brings in money, does that make it 'work'?
If what you do is unpaid, does that make it 'leisure'?

➤ Can you define what leisure is for *you*? Is it just the absence of things you don't particularly enjoy, or is it more a time when you actively do something which you do enjoy? Complete this sentence:

> For me, leisure is the time when...

➤ Make a chart like this to show how your use of leisure time has changed in the last three years:

| In my leisure time 3 years ago I used to..... | In my leisure time now I.... |
|---|---|
|  |  |

⟫ Look at the leisure pursuits of three people you know: a parent, a pensioner, and someone who has just left school. Write down what they do for enjoyment in their spare time. Do any of them:
- just seem to be resting?
- choose to do something which could be called work — whether paid or not?
- play a sport?
- meet their friends?
- socialize in pubs, clubs, cafes, discos etc.?
- go to entertainments such as gigs or cinemas?
- stay at home?
- hang around doing nothing in particular?

▶ People who are unemployed or retired usually have a lot of time to fill.
If you didn't come to school, how would you fill your day? Draw up two timetables: one of how your day is spent while you're at school, and another showing what you *would* do if you didn't have to come to school. Start from the time you get up and finish at bedtime.

| Timetable at school | Timetable if I didn't have school. |
|---|---|
| 0700 | |
| 0730 | |
| 0800 | |
| 0830 | |
| 0900 | |

❓ Does your new timetable allow you more time in bed, more time watching TV, more time spent on hobbies? What else?
What things limit what people do with their leisure?

⟫ Find out what facilities there are in your area for using leisure time. Go to the library and community centres. Get a leaflet about, or make a list of, the different classes available.

| DAY | CLASS | FEE | STARTING DATE |
|---|---|---|---|
| Mon.2.00-4.00. | History of Art | 14.15 | 14 January |
| Mon.6.30-9.00 | Pottery | 24.50 | * 14 January |
| Mon.6.30-9.00 | Stained Glass | 28.50 | * 14 January |
| Mon.6.30-9.00 | Silversmithing/Jewellery | 24.50 | * 14 January |
| Mon.7.00-8.30 | Philosophy | 11.00 | 14 January |
| Mon.7.00-9.00 | Woodcarving | 20.50 | * 14 January |
| Tues.10.00-12.30 | Portrait Painting | 23.50 | 15 January |
| Tues.10.00-12.30 | Silversmithing/Jewellery | 24.50 | * 15 January |
| Tues.10.00-12.30 | Pottery | 24.50 | * 15 January |
| Tues. 2.00-4.30 | Silversmithing/Jewellery | 17.00 | + 15 January |
| Tues.6.30-8.30 | Model Engineering | 22.00 | 15 January |
| Tues.6.00-9.00 | Car Maintenance | 18.50 | 22 January |
| | Woodwork | 24.50 | * 15 January |
| .30-9.00 | ...thing/Jewellery | 18.50 | 15 January |

What activities would particularly suit these groups of people?

> the elderly
> young mothers with children
> redundant middle-aged people
> unemployed young people
> the handicapped

What does each activity cost? Are any reductions made for people in special circumstances?

What sports facilities are available in your area? What's the farthest people might have to travel to get to their nearest:

> swimming pool
> ice rink
> BMX track?

## Your leisure now

▶ Write down all the things that you do which you regard as leisure pursuits, and all those which are not, outside school.

? Here is a list of how some people in a large city spend their time. Which do you regard as leisure?

> spending time with friends; housework; watching TV or video; reading; football; arts/crafts; staying at home; staying in bed; sewing or knitting; hanging about the streets; homework; shopping; gardening; decorating; looking after younger brother or sister; playing music; listening to music; going to the library; darts; drama; snooker; cooking; visiting friends or relatives.

Do you think an unemployed person would have a different attitude to any of these leisure activities?

## Your leisure in the future

? What things do you think will happen which will change what you do with your leisure time? What difference will the following make to you?

- leaving school
- getting your first job
- going on the dole
- moving away from the area

Many people say that in the future there will be less work; we shall all have to adjust to spending less time working, and to having more free time. Can you predict what the likely consequences will be? How do you think people will spend their time? Do you think people will get bored? Will they spend more money on amusing themselves, for example in pubs, restaurants, discos, cinemas, clubs? What might the effects of this be?

Do you do any things in school which might prepare you for a shorter working week and more leisure time? If so, what are they? Could your school do more? If so, what could it do?

# Planning and organizing an event

This section is about the process of organizing yourself, and other people, for the sort of event which before has probably been organized for you. It's not necessary to do exactly what's suggested here. These visits are only ideas. You'll probably have some better ideas yourself.

We've already looked at things that you may want to do more on your own now, rather than with your family. Going out with friends, staying with them, and maybe going on holiday, are some. But even an apparently simple journey can take quite a lot of thought and organization.

There's a group of us who are vaguely thinking that in our last year at school we could try and organize a visit to some local employers where some of us will be applying to work. But we don't really know if it's possible or how to organize it.

I wanted to go and stay with my sister. It was expensive to buy a train ticket. Then I found out I could have got one much cheaper off-peak — and that there was a coach which would have taken me to her door, practically, which was even cheaper.

We thought it would be great to have a party, with some music. But the trouble was that no one really thought about how it was going to work, or where it was going to be, or who we were going to invite. In the end it was disastrous, because hardly anyone turned up, and nothing much happened.

**?** Look at each of the stories above. For each one, say:
- what you think the best way of organizing each event would be
- what information each person would need to organize what they want to do.

Here are some events to plan. You can plan them on your own or in small groups:

**1** a day trip
**2** a visit to a factory, bank, newspaper, brewery, or any other local business. If you're in a group, you'll have to decide which event is possible in your area, and how to find out what's available.

## The day trip

This should be to somewhere within easy travelling distance of your school. Here are some ideas: a wildlife park, the sea, a shopping centre, an amusement park, your nearest sports and leisure complex, or even a day trip to the continent if you live near a port.

**»** How do you find out what there is within, say, a thirty-mile radius of your school?
How do you find out the distance to places? Which of these could help?
> the bus station
> an information centre

a travel agent
a tourist bureau
British Rail
the local paper
a street map
a road atlas of Britain

You should weigh up the advantages and disadvantages of each idea. Or you could set yourself some limits on things like cost, distance, time you're prepared to spend travelling, numbers you want to take, before starting to look at where to go.

## Travel

❓ Which of these would be the cheapest for travel?
train
taxi
hired coach or minibus
bus

Remember that you can often get special day-trip rates on trains and buses. What do you think would be a reasonable amount to spend on travel for each person?
Which do you think would be quickest?
Imagine you are booking a coach for the day. What questions will the coach office ask you? Finish these:
'Where…?
'When…?
'How many…?
How will you get people interested in the trip?
What do you think the problems might be on the day?

▶ Write an announcement to go on the notice board, advertising the trip and giving the following details:
● anything you think people should take with them — how much spending money, any warm clothes, food, and so on
● the time and place of departure
● how long you think you will be away
● the approximate cost of the trip.

Collect leaflets and advertisements about places that look interesting and worth a visit.

### A visit to a factory, bank, or other business

Most large firms have someone called a Public Relations Officer, a Personnel Officer, or a Training Officer, who might be prepared to show a party of you around, and answer your questions. Before you go, make sure you are clear about what you want to find out.

Some places have 'open days' which are specially for showing the public round the premises.

Make a list of suitable places to visit locally. Ask your Careers Officer to help, or ask people who have got jobs whether their firm shows people round.

Set out a letter to the Training Officer of Anyparts Ltd., Northtown, saying that you are hoping to arrange a visit for your class to local firms and businesses. Ask him or her if a visit is possible, and which dates are convenient. If you're not sure how to set out the letter, have a look at the section on letter writing in Chapter 2.

If you are accepted on a visit round the factory, it helps if you show an interest in what's going on. Think of some questions to ask the person who shows you round. They could be about:
- the number of employees
- whether there's a Union
- the number of young people the firm takes on every year
- where the products go — are any exported?
- what staff training there is.

A pleasant 'thank you' letter afterwards will make the firm more inclined to receive young people on visits in the future.

# Getting around

## Timetables

Timetables use the 24-hour clock. Are you happy to tell the time using that system? Check yourself and see. Write down in words what these times are, and whether it's morning (a.m.) or afternoon/evening (p.m.).

| | |
|---|---|
| 14.00 | 18.30 |
| 11.15 | 20.45 |
| 12.00 | 21.05 |
| 03.00 | 17.35 |

Using the 24-hour clock, write down the following times:

1 The time you leave home in the morning.
2 The time this lesson began.
3 The time this lesson ends.
4 The time Top of the Pops starts.
5 The time you got up this morning.
6 The time you got in last night.
7 The time you went to bed last night.

Here's a picture of a clock with the 24-hour system on it to help you.

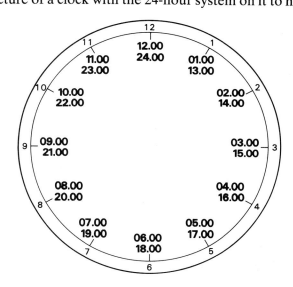

## How long?

Working out how long programmes last, or how long journeys will take, using the 24-hour clock can be confusing. Here are some examples to practise:

1 The first bus from your street to town leaves at 06.40. It gets to town at 07.15. How long is the bus journey?
2 When you come home, the bus leaves at 17.15. If it takes the same time on the return journey, what time will you get off the bus again in your street?
3 You want to be in the town centre to meet a friend at 19.30. You don't want to be late. The journey takes 35 minutes. Buses run every 15 minutes up to 18.00, then they run every 30 minutes. Write down the time of the bus you would catch.
4 You're going on the coach to visit a friend. The journey takes three and a half hours. If the coach leaves your local bus station at 15.15, what time should you tell your friend that you will arrive?

## Reading street maps

Look at map 1 which shows the centre of Coventry. Like most street maps, it's marked into squares to help you find where places are. Each square on this map represents half a mile. The squares are labelled by letters at the top and bottom, and by numbers on the right- and left-hand sides. In the index of streets and places, each entry has a reference which is made up of a letter and number. You can find where the street or place you're looking for is by following the labelled squares. For example, Eagle Street is J7.

Find the following on the map:

Greyfriars, H9                    Bus Depot, H7
Lancaster Polytechnic, J8     Rail Station, H9.

Using the system of letters and numbers, and writing the letter first, give the reference for:

Far Gosford Street
Police HQ
Bishopsgate Green
the Cathedral

What do you think the following abbreviations stand for?

Wks          Sch          Mkt

Map 2 is of Tile Hill, just west of the centre of Coventry. Find the station. Explain to someone else how to get on foot from the station to:

the Health Centre (C8)
Alderman Harris Primary School (C10)
Wickman Ltd. (A8)
the Technical College (C9).

If each square represents half a mile, how far, approximately, will each walk be from the station? How long would each walk take if you walked one mile in twenty minutes? If you wanted a more accurate calculation of the distance, how would you get it?

## Using a street map of your local town

For this exercise, you will need a street map of your local town, and a copy of a timetable for a bus route there. Now:

1 Find all the places that are mentioned on the bus timetable.
2 Pencil in the route the bus takes.

Is your street on the map? If so, can you find the roads which take you by the shortest route from your house to the following places:

the College of Further Education
the rail station
the nearest shopping precinct
the nearest police station?

On the map, find the following:

as many schools as you can        any ring roads or by-passes
the police stations                      any technical colleges.
the fire station

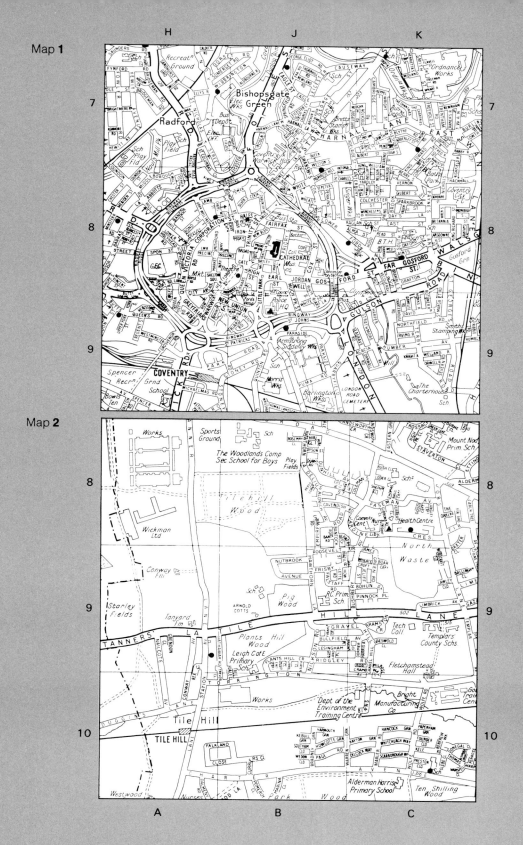

Map **1**

Map **2**

▶ Practise drawing sketch maps. They can be quite difficult to get right. One problem is that you can't give much idea of distance or scale. Try the following to start with:
- a sketch map of your school
- a sketch map of the street you live in, with any landmarks such as shops, pubs, traffic lights, bus stops
- a sketch map of your nearest shopping centre, with places that you like to go marked.

## Using a road atlas

Borrow a road atlas and look up your area of the country. Find out what the scale is — it's usually something like three or five miles to the inch.

▶ Answer the following questions:
1 What are the names of the roads which lead out West, East, South, and North from your nearest big town? The roads are named by a letter and a number, for example, A345.
2 How many big towns are within a thirty-mile radius of where you live?
3 In relation to where you live, say whether the following cities are North, North-East, East, South-East, South, South-West, West, or North-West:

      Cardiff
      Bristol
      Leeds
      Cambridge
      London
      Edinburgh

4 Which are the nearest motorways to your home?

## Planning journeys

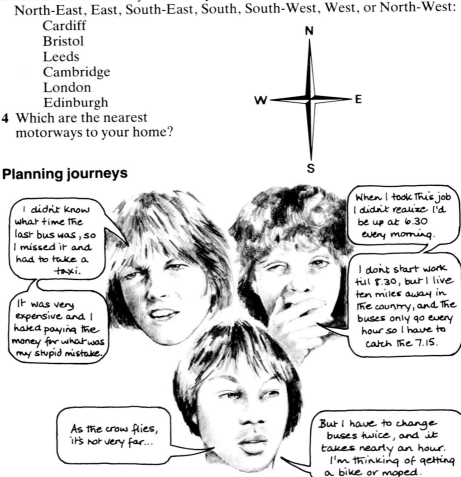

**1** Ray has to be at his job by 8 a.m. He lives a ten-minute walk from the bus stop. Buses leave on the hour, and every quarter of an hour after that. The journey takes twenty minutes, and then he has a five-minute walk to work. He must be on time, because if he arrives one minute past eight o'clock, he loses a quarter of an hour's pay.

What time should Ray leave home in order to get to work on time?
How long does Ray spend travelling each morning?
The return journey takes five minutes longer, because the traffic is always heavier. How long does he spend travelling each day?
What distance do you think Ray lives from his job? Can you suggest ways of travelling to work for Ray which would be cheaper or quicker?

**2** Carmen attends a course at a college twenty miles from her home. Sometimes a friend gives her a lift to the station, which is five minutes' drive away. She then has a half-hour train journey, and a fifteen-minute walk from the station. She likes to get to college at 8.45. Trains leave her local station at 6.45, 7.10, 7.45, and 8.10.

Which train should Carmen catch?
How long does the journey take?

### Find out about the cost of journeys yourself

Choose a place to travel to, within twenty-five miles of where you live.
How many ways of getting there could you use?
> Which would be the cheapest?
> Which would be the quickest?
> Which would be the most comfortable?

Ask at the rail station and the bus station if there are any special rates or discounts which make it cheaper to travel at certain times.

# Environment

We use the word 'environment' to describe our surroundings. Make a list of all the things that you think are covered by the word 'environment'. Ask yourself whether it covers things like:

- the sort of place you live
- the sort of place you go to school
- where you spend your leisure time
- where you go on holiday
- what your neighbourhood is like
- what your public transport is like — whether you have to travel in crowded, smoke-filled buses, for example.

For each of the things that you've listed, put down how you like it to be for you. Does your description include words like 'nice, clean, tidy, well cared for'?

**?** Whose responsibility do you think it is to look after the bits of the environment that you've identified? As we see in Chapter 5, we have public services which care for our water supply, sewage, refuse disposal and public amenities like parks; but what should the public do to look after their environment? What should *you* be doing?

What contribution do you make to caring for your environment
- at home
- at school
- in your neighbourhood?

'Pollution' means making the environment dirty and harmful. It's often used to describe the effects that some industries have on the environment. But it can also refer to smaller scale incidents. Can you think of ways in which, without meaning to, you perhaps cause harm to the environment or annoy other people? When did you last:
- play music very loudly, so that people complained?
- mend your bike on the pavement?
- let your dog or cat annoy other people?
- drop litter on the street?
- deface or destroy something?

What would your reaction be if someone complained that you had done any of the above things?
Would you feel that they:
- had a point, and thank them for telling you?
- were interfering in your life and had no right to do so?
- probably did things which annoyed you, like smoking in public places?
Would you stop what you were doing?

What things are you pleased with about your environment now, and what are you annoyed about? Try to divide it up into school, home, and neighbourhood.

## The link between people and their environment

People can have a good or bad effect on their environment. But their surroundings affect them too, perhaps causing them to behave in a particular way. Read this story about some young people who feel there isn't much for them in their area.

**'It just sort of happened . . .'**

What is your reaction to this story?

Do you feel sympathy with the young people or not?

What things might they do instead?

One of them says it would be better if they had a youth club. If they wanted to get one started, who could they contact for help?

What do you think the people whose walls were sprayed feel now about the young people who live around them?

**?** People are very sensitive to their environment, and respond to it. Even a newborn baby can respond to shapes and colours. How do you think people feel who live in areas where there is vandalism and graffiti?

Most settings have their good features and their drawbacks.

What would you say are the advantages and disadvantages of living in
      an isolated village in the country
      a heavily-populated urban area?

People can also control and influence their environment.

These two walls are in the same area. The painting was done by the members of a local school. Why do you think it has not been spoiled?

### What's your own area like?

Build up a picture of the place where you live. Get a street map of the area. Divide it up into sections. Divide your class into groups.

Each group is responsible for surveying one section.

Decide on how to record your information: through photographs, drawings, bar charts, models, tape-recorded interviews, colour-coded maps, written reports. Consider these things in the section of the map that you are working on.

**Housing**
How much of the area is residential?
What types of houses are there? Mainly flats, terraced houses, semis, or detached houses?
Do most of them seem to be owner-occupied, multi-occupation, private, or council property?
Can you roughly date the time the houses/flats were built?
Are they in a good state of repair?

**Population**
Do people live and work in the area? Do they travel to work elsewhere?
Are there people who travel into the area to work, leaving again at night?
If so, what effect does this have on the area?
Is there a 'transient' population, such as tourists or students?

**Health care**
How many Health Centres, hospitals, day-care centres for the elderly, and facilities for the disabled can you find?

**Employment and industry**
Look at the places where people work in the area. Do they work mainly in service industries, manufacturing industries, agriculture, or other industries?
Can you find evidence of growth — for example, new shopping centres or industrial development? Is there evidence of decline — for example, closed businesses and boarded-up shops?

**Education**
How many nurseries, schools, and colleges are there? Are there any adult or community education groups or classes?

**Recreation and leisure facilities**
What facilities for recreation and leisure are there? Include parks, recreation grounds, sports centres, bingo halls, cinemas, theatres, and anything else which you think appropriate.

**Community support services**
Can you find any organizations such as Housing Aid Centres, Information Centres, the Citizens' Advice Bureau, Drop-in Centres, Residents' Associations or Tenants' Associations? If so, ask them what they do.

### Traffic, parking, and public transport

What does the council's policy on traffic seem to be? Are there any pedestrian-only areas? Any one-way traffic systems? How good are car parking facilities?

How much does it cost to park your car for a day? Would a driver consider the cost to be high or low? How good is the public transport system? When do the first and last buses go each day?

### Policing

How is the area policed? Do you see police on the beat?

### Planning objectives

Try to find out from local newspapers what the planning authorities are trying to achieve for the area. Are they trying to encourage or discourage particular forms of development?

### The future

What does the future of the area seem to be?

### What do local people think?

Interview local people in the area. Find out what they think is good and bad about living or working there. Think of some specific questions to ask; for example: Do you know your local police officers? What do you think of the public transport system here? What changes would you like to see? Do you think you have adequate facilities for leisure and for your children?

## Conservation

Some people feel so strongly that parts of our environment should be preserved, that they form pressure groups to make their views known. Can you think of anything to do with the environment about which you feel strongly enough to join a pressure group or to protest publicly?

# 2 Communicating

For most people, 'communication' means talking and listening, reading and writing. But there are other ways to get a message across. Some ways don't use words at all, and yet it's quite easy to understand what the message is.

► In each of these pictures, something is being said. Make a list of the different ways in which the message is being got across.

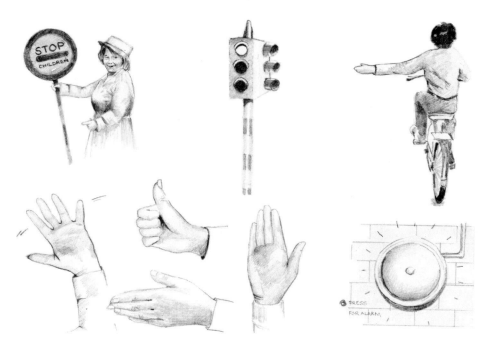

❓ Can you think of any ways in which someone has got a message across to you today without actually speaking? What did the person do?

## Communicating without words

Two ways of communicating which don't involve words are (1) creating an impression and (2) body language.

### Creating an impression

We get immediate impressions of people, and even make long-lasting judgements about them, from the way they appear to us. Things like clothes and hairstyle create effects which may or may not be intended.

**?** For each of the following pictures of the ways people dress, can you say:
- what impression you think the wearer is trying to create
- what impression it makes on you
- what impression you think it might give to an older person
- what a prospective employer might think about this person from the way he or she dresses.

**?** Are girls more concerned with their appearance than boys? Do you know boys who are
- concerned with wearing fashionable clothes
- concerned about their skin or hair
- concerned about being fat or thin, short or tall?

**▶** To find out what you think about your own appearance and attitude to clothes, finish these sentences:
1 To me clothes are…
2 I dress the way I do because…
3 I am influenced in the way I dress by…
4 When I go out for the evening my parents say I look…
5 The best thing about the way I look is…
6 The worst thing about the way I look is…
7 If my mum or dad tried to dress like me and my friends I'd think…
8 If my teacher tried to dress like me I'd think…

## Body language

The ways people use their hands and faces, and how they stand or sit, tell us something about them. How do people stand or sit if they are:
- waiting to see the dentist
- waiting for a bus
- waiting for a friend who's late
- waiting for a job interview? (Would it make a difference if there was someone else, for example a receptionist, in the same room?)

 Get a friend to mime three of the situations. Can you tell which is which?

40

**?** From the way this man is sitting, can you tell when he is (a) relaxed, (b) confident, (c) bored, (d) depressed, (e) alert, and (f) worried?

### Hands and gestures

**?** What gestures would you use to go with the following actions?
- reassuring someone
- seeing someone out of the room or house in a friendly way
- ordering someone out of the house
- a parent telling off his or her own child
- a parent telling off a neighbour's child.

### Eyes

**?** What impression do you have if someone:
- avoids looking at you and keeps their eyes fixed on the ground
- stares at you constantly
- looks past you all the time?

What sort of 'eye contact' suggests that someone is interested and listening to you?

# Talking and listening

Why are listening and talking important skills?

**?** Think about some situations where you might need to be able to:
- tell people about yourself
- ask for help
- listen carefully to what's being said
- do exactly as someone else says
- understand what's being said

Think of as many different situations as you can.

**?** Why are these skills difficult?
When do you find it easy to talk?
Ask people who know you if they think you are:
**a** quiet and a good listener
**b** someone who talks and listens
**c** a great talker who doesn't always listen
**d** someone who can't communicate.

**▶** Now see if you agree with their judgement of you. Do this short quiz:

1 At a bus stop, you are likely to begin a conversation with the person standing next to you:
   **a** always
   **b** sometimes
   **c** never
   **d** only if you know him or her.

2 At parties, you:
   **a** are happy to go and talk to people you don't know.
   **b** talk to people you don't know only with great difficulty.
   **c** talk to people you don't know only if you are with someone who does know them.
   **d** talk only to people you know.

**3** If you had to tell the doctor or careers officer about yourself you:
  **a** would be happy to go and talk on your own.
  **b** would take a friend, but do the talking yourself.
  **c** would rather someone like your mum or dad came and did the talking for you.
  **d** would go on your own even though you didn't like to.

**4** If you had an interview for a Saturday job and the employer asked you what your hobbies were, you would:
  **a** say 'I haven't got any' even though you have, just to avoid talking.
  **b** tell him and take half an hour over it.
  **c** tell him and ask what his are.
  **d** tell him briefly.

**5** Someone you don't know very well stops you in the street and tells you all about their pet hamster who's just died. You're in a hurry. Do you:
  **a** stay and listen even though it means you'll be late?
  **b** explain that you're going somewhere but ask them to come round to your house sometime?
  **c** tell them to buy a new one and rush off?
  **d** say 'I never did like hamsters anyway'?

**6** Do people often seem to say to you 'You haven't been listening to a word I've said'?
  **a** Yes, and it's true.
  **b** Yes, but you have been listening really.
  **c** Yes, but only your mum.
  **d** No, because you're good at saying 'Hm' in the right places.

**7** A good talker is someone who:
  **a** talks non-stop.
  **b** knows when to talk and when to listen.
  **c** is never boring and always knows a good joke.
  **d** gets other people talking too.

**8** A good listener is someone who:
  **a** never interrupts.
  **b** asks questions to keep the person talking.
  **c** says sympathetic things.
  **d** waits till you get to the end before saying 'Well I think you should…'.

| 1 | 2 | 3 | 4 | 5 | 6 | 7 | 8 |
|---|---|---|---|---|---|---|---|
| a 5 | a 5 | a 5 | a 2 | a 4 | a 5 | a 5 | a 4 |
| b 4 | b 4 | b 4 | b 5 | b 4 | b 4 | b 4 | b 4 |
| c 2 | c 3 | c 2 | c 5 | c 5 | c 4 | c 5 | c 3 |
| d 3 | d 2 | d 3 | d 4 | d 5 | d 5 | d 4 | d 5 |

The nearer your score is to 40, the more likely you are to talk rather than listen. Perhaps you could try to pay more attention to what people are saying to you. Around 30, and you're a good talker and listener. Nearer 20, and you're probably not the talkative type. But sometimes you may have to talk to other people. The more you practise, the easier it gets.

## Occasions when it's difficult to talk

**?** Why might it be difficult to talk:
- at a job interview?
- to a policeman?
- to your boyfriend's/girlfriend's father?
- to the family doctor?

Get a friend to play the part of the interviewer, the policeman, the father, and the doctor in each of the above situations. In the first two situations, the interviewer and the policeman start the conversations. In the last two situations, *you* must start the conversation.

**?** Can you think of some situations where you've found it difficult to talk recently? Explain to a friend exactly why it was difficult. Looking back, what could you have done to make the situation easier? What would your friend have done in the same situation?

## Tone and voice

**?** How would you react if someone you'd never met before suddenly said:
> 'Hey! You!'
> 'Excuse me.'
> 'What do you think you're doing?'
> 'Move over.'
> 'Can you please...'
> 'You're late.'
> 'Would you mind...'

Does the way they say it make a difference? How many ways are there of saying 'Do you mind?'? Try saying them out loud. How much difference does it make to your reaction if you know the person well?

What facial and hand gestures might go with each of the above to make what is said:

**a** more friendly?
**b** less friendly?

Practise saying the opening lines in these situations:
1 You're lost and you need help to find the way.
2 You're in a strange building and you need to find the toilet.
3 You want to make an appointment.
4 You're not sure if you've come to the right place.

The tone of voice you use and your attitude to the person you're talking to will often help or hinder you. Even if you're complaining or have noticed a mistake someone else has made, you can deal with it pleasantly. And you're more likely to get the complaint or mistake put right if the other person isn't thinking 'We've got a right one here'. So, with a friend, practise pleasant ways of saying the opening lines in these situations:
1 The jeans you bought in this shop have split after two weeks.
2 You think there's been a mistake in your change.
3 You notice that the person in the queue behind you is charged less for the same thing as you bought.
4 At work, someone keeps sending faulty goods down the line.

## Interview other people

Young people are often criticized for being too quiet in interviews. They tend to give short answers, like 'yes', 'no', or 'don't know'. The interviewer then feels he or she hasn't learnt very much about the young person.

With a partner, practise asking questions about each other to which a 'yes' or 'no' answer won't do.

With a partner, and using a cassette recorder if you've got one, try interviewing some people. Decide before you start what it is that you want them to tell you about — for example, what their childhood was like, what they do in their spare time, what they think of young people, how they found their first job, whether they know what facilities are available for young people in your area. When you've decided on a topic, make a list of questions you want to ask them.

After the interview, play the tape back, or look at your notes. Then answer these questions:
1 How successful were you in finding out what you wanted to know?
2 Did people answer your questions?
3 Did they stick to the point or ramble?
4 Was it easy or difficult to get them to talk?
5 What did you do to encourage them to talk?
6 What did you do to try to stop them talking?

As an interviewer, how would you have felt if you'd got these replies?:
    'I don't know really.'
    'I don't mind.'
    'I don't care.'
    'It's all the same to me.'

## Saying things clearly

Well, you go past the what-d'you-call-it on the right, or it may be on the left, and after that there's a big round thing, and it's by there.

Have you ever asked someone for directions on how to get somewhere or do something, and felt none the wiser when they'd told you? It's often difficult to give someone else instructions, even if you yourself know very well how to do whatever it is. For instance, you can get from your house to the nearest post office easily; but can you tell someone else how to do it?

It's useful to be able to describe things clearly to people. You may need to:

tell someone where to meet you

talk about yourself

describe something that's happened to you

say what happened in a road accident you saw

tell someone how to do something.

Here are some examples to practise.
Tell a partner how to:

- perform a simple task or check on a motorbike, moped, or bicycle
- cook something simple
- make something — a paper aeroplane would do
- perform a task like knitting or a sewing stitch
- get from your house to the bus station.

It'll work best if your partner doesn't know how to do the task, so that you can check how good your instructions are. Get him or her to write down or remember what he or she thinks you said, and to repeat the instructions. How accurate do you think your instructions were? Ask your partner how easy they were to understand. Did you:

repeat yourself?

miss anything out?

use words or technical terms that were difficult to understand?

talk vaguely?

Remember, this exercise is not to test your partner's memory, but your skill in communicating clearly!

## Apologizing, excusing, and explaining

Most people find apologizing or excusing themselves difficult. Can you say why? Is it something that you yourself find difficult? Is it for any of these reasons?

- for fear of being shouted at
- in case people don't believe you
- because saying sorry is difficult
- because you think it won't do any good anyway
- because it's safer to keep quiet and say nothing.

But look what happened to these people, who were too shy or scared to explain themselves — or just thought it wouldn't do any good.

**?** In each of the above situations, what could Karen, Barry, and Sam have said to make the outcome better for themselves? Do you think that they were right to keep quiet, or should they have tried to explain? Does it ever do any harm to try and explain? As you can see, you have to decide whether the result will be worse if you don't explain. What did Karen, Barry, and Sam risk losing?

With a friend, role-play the situations in which Karen, Barry, and Sam found themselves, but this time, make sure that they explain the reasons for their lateness.

Think of some occasions recently when you have apologized or excused yourself or tried to explain your mistake to someone. What was the other person's reaction? Try role-playing the situation again, with another person playing you. You will have to explain to them what it was that you were apologizing about. Then you play the person you're trying to apologize to. Do you think your partner handled it better than you did?

**?** Who do you find it most difficult to apologize to? Why?

## Listening

**?** With a friend, decide how you can tell:
- when someone is listening
- when someone is definitely not listening
- when someone is only pretending to listen.

Write down five qualities that make a good listener. How many qualities are to do with being friendly, sympathetic, and so on, and how many are to do with remembering what you're told?

In which situations would it be important to be a sympathetic or friendly listener, and in which might it be important to do as you're told?

Can you think of occasions *now* in your life when it's important for you to remember what you're told and follow instructions? Do you think that as you get older it will become more important?

At work, it is important to listen and follow instructions. Can you give five reasons why?

## How good a listener are you?

Try these exercises:

**?** 1 Ask someone to tell you some things about him or herself — it might be a good idea to ask someone you don't know all that well, so that the information is new to you. Try to remember what he or she says, and repeat them to your partner. Did you get them right? Ask your partner if you were completely right, only half right, less than half right, or completely wrong.

2 If you saw or listened to it, how much can you remember of this morning's or last night's news and weather forecast?

Ask a friend to take a cutting of a short article from a newspaper or magazine and read it to you. How much can you remember about it without looking?

3 What suggestions have you got for helping people to remember what they're told? Which of these ideas might be useful?
- making sure that the information is given in a quiet place without interruptions
- jotting down what's said
- drawing pictures or diagrams
- asking for a demonstration
- asking if you can repeat what's just been said
- if instructions on how to operate something are being given, asking if you can try out the process.

If you really can't remember and you have to ask someone to repeat what they said it can be embarrassing, but probably better than carrying on and possibly making a mistake. Practise saying things like:

I'm sorry, I'm afraid I don't understand ...

Could you repeat that please?

Could you say that again slowly?

Can you think of any more expressions you could use?

48

# Phones

We haven't got a phone at home and I'm not sure how to use a call box. It's not the sort of thing people teach you. They just assume you know.

Andy

I don't mind talking to people face to face, but I hate using the phone. You can't tell what they're like, and they always sound snooty.

Chris

If you have doubts about using the phone, have a look at this section.
If you feel happy about using the phone, maybe you could help some of the others in the group.

➤➤ Try and find out why some people dislike phones. Gather as many reasons as you can. Do they fall into the same categories as Andy's and Chris's problems? Andy's problems are practical — he wants to know how the machine works. Chris's are more to do with her feelings about the phone — she sounds worried and a bit nervous. Maybe if Chris were sure about how to use the phone, and what to say, she'd practise a bit more and become more confident. First we'll look at the practical part.

## How to use the phone

### Money

49

Old-style call-boxes take only 10p pieces. New ones take 2p, 10p, and 50p pieces. In some call-boxes, you can now use a plastic credit card, which you buy from newsagents. It might be a good idea to buy one if you've got a lot of calls to make — for example when you're enquiring about jobs — but it might also encourage you to stay on the phone longer and so waste money.

Phone calls from public call-boxes are most expensive between 8 a.m. and 6 p.m. from Monday to Friday. Phone calls from private phones cost most from 8 a.m. to 1 p.m. (peak), cost less from 1 p.m. to 6 p.m. (standard), and are cheapest after 6 p.m.

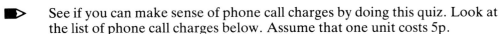 See if you can make sense of phone call charges by doing this quiz. Look at the list of phone call charges below. Assume that one unit costs 5p.

**1** What can you use to pay for calls from a call box?
**2** When are phone calls cheapest from a call box?
**3** How much time do you get for 10p on:
   **a** a local call at cheap rate?
   **b** a call to somewhere more than 56 kilometres away at standard rate?
   **c** a call to somewhere less than 56 kilometres away at cheap rate?
**4** How far away are the places to which calls are charged at rate **b**?
**5** How much does it cost to dial the Irish Republic for three minutes at peak time?
**6** How much does it cost to dial somewhere more than 56 kilometres away for five minutes at cheap rate?

## Phone call charges

| Dialled calls Local calls | | Approx. cost to the customer incl. VAT | | | | | Time for one unit |
|---|---|---|---|---|---|---|---|
| | | 1 min | 2 mins | 3 mins | 4 mins | 5 mins | |
| Local    L | Cheap | 5p | 5p | 5p | 5p | 5p | 8 mins |
| | Standard | 5p | 5p | 11p | 11p | 16p | 2 mins |
| | Peak | 5p | 11p | 11p | 16p | 22p | 1 min 30 secs |

## National and Irish Republic calls

| | | | | | | | |
|---|---|---|---|---|---|---|---|
| Calls up to 56 km (35 miles) *a* | Cheap | 5p | 5p | 11p | 11p | 16p | 2 mins |
| | Standard | 11p | 16p | 22p | 32p | 38p | 45 secs |
| | Peak | 11p | 22p | 32p | 43p | 54p | 30 secs |
| Calls over 56 km (35 miles) *b* | Cheap | 11p | 16p | 22p | 27p | 38p | 48 secs |
| | Standard | 16p | 32p | 49p | 65p | 81p | 20 secs |
| | Peak | 22p | 43p | 65p | 86p | £1.08 | 15 secs |
| Calls to the Irish Republic from Great Britain and the Isle of Man | Cheap | 22p | 43p | 65p | 86p | £1.08 | 15 secs |
| | Standard | 43p | 81p | £1.24 | £1.62 | £2.05 | 8 secs |
| | Peak | 43p | 81p | £1.24 | £1.62 | £2.05 | 8 secs |

### No money?

If you have no money and need to phone someone, you could try asking them if they'll pay for the call. Dial 100. The operator will say 'Operator services'. Before you give the number, you say 'transfer charge call please', or 'reverse charge call please'. The operator likes to know this first; then you can give the number you want.

 Practise in twos asking for a transfer charge call. One of you is the operator, the other a penniless caller. When the person you want to talk to picks up the phone, the operator will ask if he or she will pay for the call. If the answer is 'yes', the operator will put you through; or you may be asked to give your name first. Calling reverse charges is expensive for the person who takes the call, so don't expect to make these calls to people you don't know very well.

**Freefone** means that you can make the call without paying. Some firms or agencies providing a service can be dialled Freefone. You dial 100 for the operator, and say that you want Freefone, followed by the number.

## Dialling

Every phone number has an exchange before it. For example, in the number Wigan 85718, Wigan is the exchange. What is the exchange for the area where you live? Is it the same as the exchange for your school? (It may not be, if you travel a long way to school.)

Find some numbers in the telephone directory which have the same exchange as you. If you wanted to phone these numbers, you would simply dial the number. You would not need to use a code first.

### Dialling codes

 To dial numbers which are outside your own exchange, you need to dial a code first. Look in the code book, and find the codes for Cardiff, Newcastle, Coventry, Manchester, and Brighton. Find the codes of three places which are within thirty miles of your home. If you're looking up codes and numbers to make a call, you might find it difficult to remember them both, especially since they'll be in different books. Write them down on a piece of paper. Write the code first, then the number you want to dial.

 Write down the code and number for:
> Southampton 051123
> Norwich 064451
> Gateshead 032561
> Newport (Gwent) 0266789

## Looking up telephone numbers

If you want to phone someone and don't know their number, you can look in the telephone directory; in the *Yellow Pages*, if it's the number of a firm or service; or you can ring Directory Enquiries and ask them to find you the number. People who aren't happy about using the directory like to ring the operator, but obviously it's a good idea to be able to look things up for yourself.

**Telephone directories**

The names of subscribers (that is, people with phones) are printed in alphabetical order of their surname or business.

Look for the names of ten people you know in the directory. Are they there? If you find a lot of people with the same name, look for the initials of the person you want. They will also be in alphabetical order.

Some numbers can be tricky to find, because instead of being listed under their own names, they come under the name of the local authority or some other organization. For example, the Unemployment Benefit Office comes under 'Employment, Department of'; The Department of Health and Social Security comes under 'Health and Social Security, Department of'; the Careers Office comes under the name of your City or County Council's Education Department; Social Services comes under the name of your City or County Council. Your doctor could be in the directory under his or her own name, but if he or she belongs to a group practice at a health centre, the health centre's number will be under the name of your county, followed by 'Health Authority'.

**Yellow Pages**

This is a list of firms and services, grouped under headings. The headings are listed alphabetically, and go from Abbattoirs to Zoos. The firms are then listed alphabetically under each group. Try to find the number of:

a dog kennels
a taxi service
a Chinese takeaway
a TV repair person
a solicitor
a bank
a window cleaner

Sometimes people aren't listed where you'd expect them to be. Try to think of another name for what they do, or use the cross-reference section at the back of the Yellow Pages. For example, if your doctor is in the Yellow Pages, he'll be listed under 'Physicians and Surgeons'. Confusing, isn't it? And not easy to remember if you're in a hurry. Try to get familiar with the directory and the Yellow Pages by looking up the numbers of as many organizations as you can think of.

To help you keep track of useful numbers, start to make your own personal telephone directory, putting the names in alphabetical order.

### Using Directory Enquiries
If you haven't got a phone book handy, or if you want to know the number of someone who lives outside the area covered by the book, you can ask the operator to look it up for you. Dial 192. The operator will ask you the name of the town you want, and then the name of the people, their initials and address.

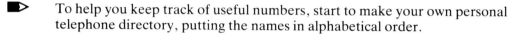

In pairs, role-play asking the operator for various numbers. You'll need a pencil and paper again.

## What to say?

With luck, you've now found a phone box that works, you've got enough money, and you have the code and number to dial ready. You pick up the receiver, and get the dialling tone. If it's an old-style phone, you dial first and then put in the money. If it's a new phone, you put the money in first and then dial. Someone answers . . .

**?** Then what? How do you actually start off? Have a look at the way these people started their conversations. Which do you think are good and which bad? Why?

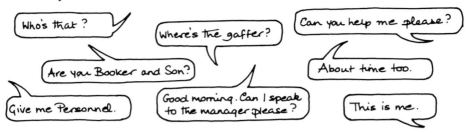

**☺** In a small group, decide how you would say the opening line in these situations:
1 You're phoning the Citizens' Advice Bureau to ask for help with an accommodation problem.
2 You're phoning the local newspaper to place an advertisement selling your old bike.
3 You're phoning an advertiser who is selling his old bike.
4 You're phoning to make an appointment with your doctor.
5 You're phoning the bus company to see if anyone has handed in the books you left on the bus.
6 You're phoning in reply to an advertisement for a babysitter.
7 You're phoning to ask for further details of a job advertised in today's local newspaper.

For each of the above situations, role-play the whole call. Do this exercise in threes; you need the caller, the person who takes the call, and an observer. The observer rates the caller out of ten, judging his or her manner, and whether he or she made the call well. The person who receives the call should be helpful and pleasant. Swap roles so that each person has a chance to be a caller.

## Finishing off

How do you remember all the information you're given on the phone?

Noting down the important things that are said is a good idea; so is going over the information again just to check. Then how do you finish the conversation?

Practise ways of saying thank you and goodbye. How many ways can you think of? Are some not suitable for use on the phone, unless you're talking to someone you know really well?

### Wrong numbers

Sometimes you dial a number, expecting a friend to answer, and you get the coal-man instead. If the person who answers the phone starts by telling you his or her number, you will usually realize there's been a mistake.
With a friend, practise what you'd say in the following situations. How would you find out if you'd got the right number or not? What would you say if you found out it was the wrong number?

1 You think you've dialled Winsford 2522, but the person who answers the phone says 'Winsford 2422'.
2 You've dialled the number for the local Further Education College. The person who answers simply says 'Hello'.
3 You've dialled the number of a firm offering a Saturday job. The person who answers says 'John Edwards'. The firm is called Brown and Brown.
4 You aren't sure if you've got through to the right number, because you didn't hear what the person answering the phone said.

If you keep on getting the wrong number, but you think you've dialled correctly, there may be a fault. Dial 100 and tell the operator. You probably won't be charged for the call then. What would you say to the operator to explain that you keep getting the wrong number?

### Ansaphones

Ansaphones are recording machines which intercept your call and take a message on a cassette. People who are out a lot of the time have them. Why might it be important for someone to have an ansaphone? What sort of people would have them?

Ansaphones are useful, because you can leave your name and number. The person you want to speak to will probably call you back when he or she gets in. Sometimes the ansaphone will give you a message, like where to contact the person you want.

### Using ansaphones

What would you do if this happened: the family washing-machine has broken down, and your mum has told you to phone the washing-machine repair man. When you do, you get a recorded message which says: 'I'm sorry I was out when you called. If you leave your name, address, and telephone number, I shall contact you when I get home. Please speak when you hear the tone. Bleeeep.'

You might feel so panicked by hearing a recorded message that you simply put the phone down and tell your mum the man was out. Or you could try to leave a message anyway, hoping that you remembered all the information he asked you to leave. Best of all, perhaps, you could ring off, think out what to say, and phone back when it's clear in your mind.

So now, practise saying to someone your name, address, and phone number, and leave them a brief message. If you have one, try speaking into a cassette recorder, and play it back. What did you sound like? Were you clear? Could you hear yourself?

### The long wait

HELLO, YOU'RE THROUGH NOW, HELLO.

Occasionally, when you phone large busy firms or departments, they have to put you through to someone in particular. The person who answers the call in the first place (called the switchboard operator) will ask you what you're calling about, or which extension you want, or the name of the person you want to speak to, and then put you through. It may take a long time. You may have to keep telling people what it is you want, while they try to sort out who should deal with it. Be patient. If you think you've been totally forgotten, ring off and try again.

If you get hold of someone who can help you, ask for their name. Then, if you have to phone back again, you can ask to speak to that person; with luck, he or she will remember you and what you want.

Practise asking people what their name is. Tricky, isn't it? You can't really say 'What's your name?' without sounding rude. Perhaps say something like 'Can you tell me your name please, in case I have to call again?' Ask them if they have an extension number, too.

### Answering the phone for other people

In which of these situations would you answer the phone? You are the only person there.
1 You're babysitting for your friend's mum and dad.
2 You're in a shop. The assistant has just gone to get something from the back.
3 You go for an interview for a job. They leave you alone in a waiting room for a few minutes and the phone goes.
4 You get the job, which is stacking shelves on Saturdays. On your first day, you're in the staff room, and the phone goes.

### Taking messages

In the situations above, the phone call almost certainly wasn't for you — though the first one might have been. What would you have done if the following conversation had taken place when you answered the phone?

Think what you would say to Bill when you saw him. What would you put if you had to write the message down?

# Letters

Do you ever write letters, or do you avoid it if you can? Would you rather use the phone than write to someone?

Letters are useful when:
- you don't want to talk to someone in person
- you want to approach someone formally
- you want to play for time
- you want to say something difficult or important
- you want what you say to be 'on record' — in which case it's a good idea to keep a copy of what you sent
- you feel so cross or upset about something that you don't trust yourself to speak.

**?** Think of an occasion on which you might have to write each of the above types of letter. Which would you say is the most difficult to write?

Think of all the reasons why we write fewer letters now than fifty or a hundred years ago. Are we more likely to regard letter-writing as an effort or chore now?

Here are some reasons people gave for not liking to write letters. Do you feel the same way?

Do you think that you might have to write letters in the future? Organizations such as the Inland Revenue and the Department of Health and Social Security like to have certain things in writing, though they are helpful and send you forms to fill in. When you come to applying for jobs or courses, you may have to write a letter or fill in a form. Some jobs are got by word of mouth and a formal or informal interview. But if you do have to write a letter to an employer or college, it will give a good impression from the start if your letter is right.

## Some hints and suggestions

- Always expect to make mistakes the first time. Write a rough copy first.
- Even if you think your handwriting is really bad, don't type the letter or get someone else to write it.
- People usually prefer to receive letters on unlined paper.
- Small mistakes can be corrected with liquid paper.
- If you are worried about your spelling or the way you've put your sentences together, get someone to check your first attempt, then write it out again if necessary.

**?** Employers receive many letters from young people asking about jobs. They can usually tell a lot about the person who's writing. If you were an employer, what would you be looking for in a letter? Think of at least five things. What would the following tell you about the writer?

1 Your name and the name of the firm are misspelt.
2 The letter has many crossings-out.
3 You can see at least six silly spelling mistakes.
4 The letter is very long and repeats itself.
5 The advertisement for the job stated quite clearly what the successful applicant would have to do when he or she started work. The applicant doesn't seem to have read or remembered what was in the advertisement.

**?** Here is a badly written letter. How many mistakes can you find?

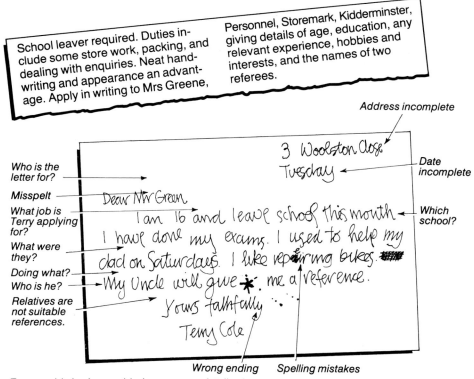

Terry could also have added some more details about
when he was available for interview, and why he wants the job.

Now look at this letter, which shows you how to set out a letter applying for a job and what to include.

your address ❶

The date

The name of the person to whom you are writing ❷
Their position in the firm
The firm's address

Dear ❸
    I am applying for the position of ❹ advertised in ❺
on ❻
    I am ❼ years old and left school in ❽ with
examination passes in the following subjects ❾ .

    Since leaving school I have been on a Government youth
Training Scheme in which I ❿

    My hobbies are ⓫

    I am interested in the job because ⓬

    I am available for interview at any time.

❸ and ❸ have agreed to provide a reference for me.

yours ⓮
⓯

1  Don't put your name here.
2  Get it right! Check with the advertisement.
3  If you don't know the person's name, put Sir/Madam.
4  Name the job.
5  The paper you saw the advertisement in.
6  The date the advertisement appeared.
7  Your age.
8  The date you left school or will leave school.
9  Examinations sat and results if you know them.
10  If this applies, say a bit about what you did.
11  Mention any that might be relevant to the job.
12  Only put a good reason.
13  The names and addresses of your referees (see p.64).
14  'Sincerely' if you wrote the person's name at the top; 'faithfully' if you put 'Dear Sir/ Madam'.
15  Sign your name and print it clearly underneath.

➤ If you had to write the following letters, what would be the most important things to include? Make a list.

1 A letter to a firm asking if they have any vacancies for which you'd be suitable.

2 A letter to the manager of an electrical shop complaining about a faulty radio which you bought from him.

3 A letter in response to the following job advertisement:

> School leaver wanted to help in busy kitchen. Must be clean and tidy. Some lifting. Write in the first instance to: The Manager, The Three Pheasants, Coleford, giving details of age, education, relevant experience, hobbies, and the names of two referees.

4 A letter to Mr Jones, 10 Bryn Mawr Avenue, Caerphilly, reserving a holiday cottage in Wales for a week and enclosing a deposit.

## Openings and endings

There are right ways and wrong ways of starting and closing letters. Some people notice whether you've done it correctly, and might take it into account if they are considering you for a job.

If you know the name of the person to whom you are writing, you should use it in your opening. It's better than 'Dear Sir' or 'Dear Madam'. If you have used the person's name, then you should sign the letter 'Yours sincerely'.

If you don't know the name of the person you're writing to (if, for example, it's 'The Secretary') then use 'Dear Sir or Madam'. In that case, you must end the letter 'Yours faithfully'.

## Drafting and rough copies

Writing is very difficult; hardly anyone gets even a short letter right first time. But once you've got it right, it's easier the next time. So try writing the letters listed above. They don't have to be long ones. When you've finished them, keep the ones to do with job applications to refer to in the future. Once you've left, it's easy to forget the correct name and address of the school, and the exact date of when you were there. You will need these when applying for jobs in the future.

### Selling yourself in a letter

If you're applying for a job, it's likely that your letter will be one of many received by the employer. This means you have to convince the employer of why *you* are the person he's looking for. You have to talk about your good points, and persuade him of your interest in the job.

The trouble is that some people are worried that they might sound conceited, and so they don't always make the best of themselves.

Have a look at the phrases and sentences below, and decide whether you think they would look good in a letter to an employer:

1 Give me the job as I've nothing else to do.
2 I have spent my Saturdays working in a greengrocer's for the last six months, and really liked the work.
3 I want to work in your place because my sister's there.
4 I'm sure you'll agree that I am ideal for the job.
5 Although I have not had a job before, I am very interested in this sort of work.
6 I think I am very good with people and would enjoy meeting them.

Write one sentence about yourself that describes one or two of your good points.

## Forms

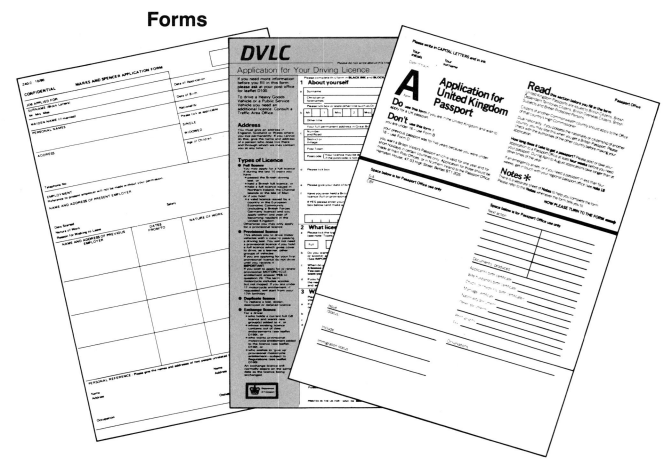

There are good things and bad things about forms when you are applying for jobs.

## The good things

1 The employer has decided what information he wants from you; he provides the spaces, and all you have to do is fill them in properly.
2 The same things usually come up on application forms. Once you've got used to them, it's fairly easy to get them right.
3 There may be a space for you to say why you want the job, or why you want to work for this particular firm, but apart from that, you won't have to write in sentences. So you needn't worry too much about whether your English is correct.

## The bad things

1 They usually only give you one form, so you have to get it right first time, unless you remember to photocopy it first.
2 They may use some phrases or expressions which are strange to you.
3 Some firms have only one form, for whatever level of entry; you may find yourself filling in the same form as someone applying for the post of deputy manager. In that case, some of the questions will seem odd, and difficult to answer.

Last year, when I was fifteen, I applied for a traineeship with a local firm. They sent me a very long form to fill in. One of the things they wanted was the names of two people who weren't relatives, who had known me well for at least six years. Since I'd only been living in this area for three years, and had lost touch with the people where I used to live, I found that very difficult.

4 If you have phoned in response to a job advertisement, you may be asked to go for an interview straight away. It can then be off-putting if they present you with a form and ask you to fill it in on the spot.

## What they ask for

These are the things which you usually have to give on a form:
- your full name (that usually means your Christian or first names and surname) and title (Mr, Mrs, Miss, or Ms)
- your permanent address
- your address for correspondence if it's different from your permanent address
- your age and/or date of birth
- the name of a parent or guardian and his/her address
- your sex
- your nationality (put 'British' rather than 'English' or 'Welsh')
- your marital status (single, married, widowed, divorced, or separated)
- number of children and their ages
- schools attended with dates
- examinations taken, with results if known
- any other qualifications or skills
- previous work experience, including part-time or holiday jobs and voluntary work

- your hobbies and interests
- the details of any serious illnesses or disabilities
- your current state of health
- the names and addresses of two referees. **A referee** is someone who knows you well, who is not related to you. The employer may want to ask him or her about your suitability for the job. Teachers, youthworkers, priests, and doctors make good referees; but any adult person whom you know and trust will do. It's important to ask them first, and perhaps to tell them what sort of job it is you're applying for, so that if they are approached by the employer, they can put forward a good case for you.

The form may also ask you to state why you are applying for the job.

Some of the things won't apply to you yet — like the number of children. To show the employer that you've read the form and not missed any sections, you could fill in 'does not apply' to these bits.

## Some traps

Some forms come with instructions at the top; some come with instructions at the bottom. Read the whole form first before you fill it in.

- It might tell you to use only black ink (probably because they want to photocopy it).
- It might tell you to use capital letters throughout.
- Under 'name', it might say 'surname first'.
- The response to 'marital status' is not 'yes' or 'no', but one of the words in brackets beside it in the list above.

How can you make it easier?

1 A good way is to ask for two forms, so that if you mess one up, you can have another chance. Or you could photocopy the first one and practise on the duplicate.

2 The other way is to become really confident at writing the information you're asked for.

▶ Practise by designing your own application form. Make it large enough for someone to fill in all the details you ask for. Think about how much space you need to give for 'schools attended', or 'examinations taken'. It'll be much greater than the space you give for 'name' or 'date of birth'. Refer back to the list of information that employers usually ask for, so that you can decide what to put on your form.

When you've designed it, hand it to someone else to fill in. You fill in the one that he or she designed.

- Did you find any bits difficult?
- Was the design of the forms good?
- How neat does your completed form look?
- How many crossings-out are there?

If you are returning the form by post, you need to make sure that you know who to send it to. It's a good idea to enclose a 'covering letter', that is, a short letter saying that you are enclosing an application form 'for the post of...', and say what the job is.

# Other ways people communicate with us

All the ways of communicating that we've looked at so far — talking, listening, writing, and gesturing — are personal. They involve you and a small number of other people. They are generally two-way communications: that is, you expect to give and get a response. But some communications can be described as being only one-way. These consist of information coming *to* you. You're not expected to make a reply, though you may behave in a particular way as a result of having seen or heard the information. For example, you may firmly decide never to smoke after seeing a programme on the dangers of cigarettes.

❓ Do you think the following communications are two-way or one-way? That is, are you required, or able, to make a response to them?
1 A letter from your local community association inviting you to an open meeting.
2 An advertisement for a new bike magazine.
3 Top of the Pops.
4 Reading the *Daily Mirror*.
5 A fire alarm going off in school.
6 A traffic light showing red.
7 A lesson where you're allowed to ask questions.
8 A lecture from the local RSPCA on the care of animals.
9 Instructions on how to make a cake.

❓ How much chance do we have to talk back to newspapers, magazines, the television, and advertisers?
Have you ever felt that you would like to be able to say what you think to these media, or doesn't it matter to you?

The rest of this chapter looks at three ways in which we receive information, and the effect these media have on us: television, newspapers and magazines, and advertising.

## Television

**?** Is television important to your age group? Answer these questions:
1 Compare the amount you watch now to the amount you watched when you were ten or eleven. Is it more or less? Can you explain why?
2 Do you watch more or less television than your parents?
3 If it's less, is this because they decide what programmes to watch, and you don't like them?
4 How much television do you watch each day?
5 What proportion of your leisure time does this come to?
6 If you could devise your ideal evening's viewing, what programmes would it consist of?

Ask someone to estimate how much time they spend watching television. Then ask them to tell you in detail which programmes they watched during the last week. Or ask them to keep a record for a week. Work out how much of their leisure time they spend watching television. Does it surprise them?

### What people think about television

➡ Make three columns on a piece of paper. Head them 'Agree', 'Disagree', and 'Don't know'. Write each comment in the column where you think it should go. Compare your list with someone else's.

## Newspapers

➡ Write down what you think the purpose of a newspaper is.
Here are the reasons some people gave for reading a paper:

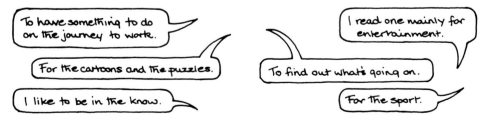

Were your reasons like any of those above?

One of the main purposes of newspapers is to inform, but what do you think they should tell us about?
Do you think it should cover any of these things? If so, why?
- what's going on abroad
- decisions that the government makes which affect us
- what the Royal Family is doing
- what the stars of Coronation Street do in their spare time
- the private lives of politicians
- crimes
- social disturbances like riots
- discoveries in science and medicine
- figures about unemployment, poverty, housing, and other social conditions
- industrial news and strikes
- fashion
- what's going on in the world of pop music
- sport

Can a newspaper inform in ways that TV and radio can't? If so, how?

### Comparing newspapers
The newspapers we have in this country are usually divided up into 'quality' papers and 'tabloids'. The quality papers are *The Times*, *The Daily Telegraph*, and *The Guardian*. Can you name some papers which are tabloids?

In groups, collect three daily newspapers for the same day.
Then answer these questions:
1 Which paper is easiest to read?
2 Which paper has most pictures?
3 Which contains most foreign news?
4 Does any of them contain an advice page?
5 Which one would you choose to read? Why?

### Values, judgements, and overtones
(If you're not sure what 'values' and 'judgements' are, look at Chapter 8.)

Do papers reflect the values of the people who read them? What values or judgements do you think lie behind these headlines?

# ROW OVER SUPPLEMENTARY BENEFITS
**BOSSES GET HUGE RISE**  **VIOLENT CRIME ON THE INCREASE**
# Health Service cut again
**BLACKS IN RIOTS AGAIN**
**HUNDREDS IDLE IN DISPUTE OVER PAY** **'NO TO GYPSIES** **Over three million on dole**

▶▶ Look again at the three papers you bought. Find one story which is reported in all three. Are there any differences in the three reports?
You might consider:
- any difference in the facts
- the amount of detail given
- the aspect of the story which the paper chooses to concentrate on
- any sympathy or value judgement which the article suggests.

❓ Does each paper appear to have a viewpoint on young people, black people, the old, women, the unemployed, the police, or protest groups?
Does each paper seem to assume things about its readers? For example, political views, type of job, level of income, interests and hobbies?

### Bias
How easy is it to report facts without bias; that is, without giving more weight to one side of the story or another, and without allowing your personal opinion to affect what you write? Very often, stories can only be written on the basis of what people say; and two people may say very different things about the same incident. Take, for example, this story about a disagreement between parents and their daughter.

Tracy's parents are increasingly worried about the time she comes in at night. They are afraid she's got in with a bad lot, and they think that she smokes and drinks. One night she didn't come in until half past eleven, although they had told her to be in by half past ten. There was a long row, during which they forbade Tracy to go out with her friends again, and threatened to stop her pocket money. They said they were doing this in order to protect her from habits that could get her into trouble. Tracy says that she tried to phone them that night to explain that she would be late because of missing the bus. But the phone was out of order, and it took her a long time to walk home. She says she was only at her girlfriend's house anyway, that she hardly ever drinks and doesn't smoke. All she wants to do is to enjoy herself, but her parents don't understand her, don't trust her, and don't believe her.

▶ Write two accounts of this story, one from the parent's point of view, and one from Tracy's point of view. Are the stories very different? Which one do you feel inclined to believe? Which one would your parents believe?

❓ Can you think of a situation which has happened to you where your version of what happened was completely different from someone else's?

### Magazines
▶▶ Bring in one magazine of your choice that is aimed at girls of your age, and one aimed at boys. Make a table to compare them. You might consider:
- the number of stories and their subject matter
- the number of factual articles and their subject matter
- what readers' letters are about
- whether there is an advice page, and if so, what the problems are about

❓ What does each magazine assume about its readers' interests and ambitions? Do you agree with these assumptions?

## Advertisements

**?** How many times a day do you think you see an advertisement? Try and count them, don't guess. What advertisements have you seen today? What were they for?

Would you say that advertisements influence you
>greatly?
>only occasionally?
>hardly at all?
>not at all?
>you can't tell how much they influence you?

**?** Can you think of something that you have done or bought as a result of an advertisement? For example, do public service announcements about road safety make you more aware of safety on the road?
Can you remember ever choosing *not* to do or buy something because the advertisement annoyed you so much?

The aim of most advertisements is to get people to part with their money. Clearly, young people, especially those who are at school or unemployed, have less money than older people with jobs. Which adverstisements can you think of that are aimed at your age group? Make a list. What sort of price is each thing? Which advertisements are aimed at your parents, to persuade them to buy things for you?
Now try and think of five advertisements that are aimed at the whole family, five which you think are aimed at men in particular, and five which are aimed at women.

Who are these slogans aimed at?
>Bright young people choose…
>Because mum knows best, she chooses…
>For the man of property and the woman of taste…
>Because you love your dog, you buy…
>Give your child a good start in life…

Some advertisements work by selling something else with the product; that is, they suggest that people who buy the product either have or will gain certain qualities. What do you think of the mums, dads, and children in advertisements? They never seem to have rows; no-one minds about dirt or washing or breakages. The advertisement seems to imply that you will have this happy life-style if you buy the product. Can you think of advertisements which make you think 'I wish I were like that'? Which ones do you think make your mum or dad feel 'I wish I could be like that'?

Look at these pictures from advertisements. What else are they selling apart from the product? What image or lifestyle do they suggest?

**Advertising Standards**

By law, advertisements have to be legal, decent, honest, and truthful, and you can complain if you think they aren't.

# DO SOME ADVERTISERS GO TOO FAR TO ATTRACT YOUR ATTENTION?

The Advertising ✓ Standards Authority.
If an advertisement is wrong, we're here to put it right.

ASA Ltd, Brook House, Torrington Place, London WC1E 7HN.

❓ Which of these statements do you think might possibly be truthful, and which obviously could not be truthful?

1 Adds years to your life.
2 Makes you look younger.
3 Washes whiter.
4 Washes whitest.
5 Removes wrinkles.
6 Keeps wrinkles at bay.
7 Builds up muscles.
8 Will make you stones lighter.

❓ Cigarette advertisements in particular link the product to a way of life or an image. The advertisers cannot say that smoking is healthy or will make you live longer, since this is obviously a lie. Collect examples of cigarette advertisements; what do they imply will happen to you as a result of smoking?

Cigarettes can't be advertised on television, and yet pipe tobacco can. Why do you think this is?

▶ Collect six other advertisements, from magazines or newspapers. Stick them on a piece of paper. Beside them, answer these questions:

1 How much information does the advertisement give you about the product?
2 What does it also suggest will happen as a result of buying the product?
3 Does the advertisement have any appeal to sex, snobbery, anti-snobbery, or status?
4 How many mention price?
5 How many make use of current trends in fashion and personalities from television or pop music? Why do you think they do this?

When you buy a product, what qualities make you choose one in particular?

# 3 Money

## Budgeting

'To budget' is to write down how much money comes in, and how much money is spent. Individuals and families budget to see what they can afford to spend money on, and to make sure they don't get into debt. The Chancellor of the Exchequer presents an annual budget to the House of Commons, which explains what money the government is going to spend, and where the money will come from for the next year.

 Ask several people you know how they manage their money. Don't ask people you don't know very well, and don't ask them about actual sums. It's rude, and they might be offended. Just ask them if they keep a record of what their income is and what they spend, and what they do when big bills come in. Do they put aside a bit of money for expenses each week? How do they save for big things like holidays, Christmas, or winter clothes?

### Why budget?

It's the only way to keep an eye on your money. It's particularly important if:
- you are trying to live off a small income
- you've just started living away from home
- you've got a home and family to look after
- you're trying to save for something, especially if it's something big like a deposit for a house
- you run your own business, or you work for yourself; you may have to show your accounts to the Inland Revenue when they are working out your tax

- you pay for things by cheque or credit card; if you don't record what you've spent, you can easily get overdrawn or exceed your credit limit
- you want to be thought of as credit-worthy and able to handle money, in case you want to go to the bank for a loan to buy something big like a car.

**?** What do *you* think are the advantages and disadvantages of budgeting?

## Budgeting your present income

That means counting up all the money that comes to you (this is called **income** or **credit**) and then counting up all the money that you spend (this is called **outgoings**, **expenses**, or **debit**).

**?** Where does your money come from at the moment? Any of these?
> a fixed allowance or pocket money
> a part-time job
> occasional gifts at Christmas and birthdays
> occasional odd jobs done for people, e.g. babysitting and car-washing
> making and selling things

Or do you have other sources of money?

**➤** Write down how much money you can be sure of having each week. Now write down what money you think you spend each week. Write it down under headings, such as fares, clothes, sweets and drinks, lunches, entertainment, magazines, books, and so on. How sure are you about how much things cost?

Which of the things on your list do you regard as essentials, and which are things that you could do without? Does anything surprise you about what you've written down? Finish this sentence:
> 'I was surprised to find that . . .'

**?** In a household of mother, father, and three children aged nine, twelve, and sixteen, what items do you think the family regards as essential, and what do you think they regard as luxuries? Will each member of the family have different ideas about what is 'essential'? What big items will they have to save for?

## Contributing to the family budget

How much do you think young people should pay their parents for their keep, once they've started earning? What should these people pay?
1 Robina is sixteen and has just started a job from which she brings home £55 per week.
2 Ted is still training and earns £38 per week.
3 Mary has no job as yet and is on supplementary benefit.

Can you write the amount you think each person should pay as a percentage of their income? Is it roughly 25%, 33%, or 50%? Most households spend about one quarter (25%) of their income on accommodation, one quarter on food, and use the remainder for everything else. If Robina, Ted, and Mary are getting food as well as accommodation at home, should they pay half of their income to their parents?

## How do other people manage?

Look at how other people have to budget their money. This is Vicki's story:

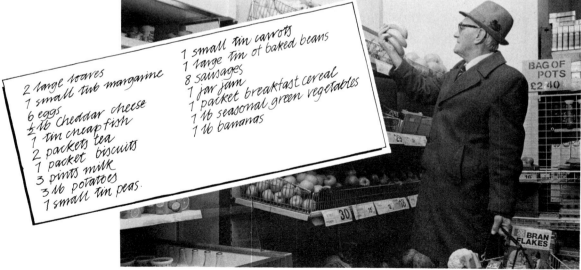

I was lucky. I moved here to find a job, got one, and somewhere to live too. But my take-home pay from the café is £39 per week, and my rent is £23 per week.

Fortunately my boss realizes it's hard to manage on a low wage and he gives us two meals a day.

I spend £4 a week on bus fares, though sometimes if I'm broke, I hitch. Gas and electricity are paid by meter. In winter I seem to use 50p a day on each. I think the meter is set high.

One of the reasons my job is low paid is that we get a lot of tips; you can't predict how much but it could be £8 or £10 in a good week.

➡ Write down Vicki's total income, from wages and tips. Write down the expenses she mentions. How much does she have left in a week? What other things would she want to buy with this money?

Fred is a pensioner who lives alone in a council flat. He lives on supplementary benefit and small amounts of other income, which come to £32 a week. His rent and rates are paid for. He is quite good at looking after himself, and always cooks himself a hot meal every day, usually at tea-time. He gets help from Meals on Wheels, and his sister-in-law will sometimes bring him a meal she's cooked.

This is Fred's shopping list for one week:

2 large loaves
1 small tub margarine
6 eggs
½ lb Cheddar cheese
1 tin cheap fish
2 packets tea
1 packet biscuits
3 pints milk
3 lb potatoes
1 small tin peas
1 small tin carrots
1 large tin of baked beans
8 sausages
1 jar jam
1 packet breakfast cereal
1 lb seasonal green vegetables
1 lb bananas

BAG OF POTS £2 40

➡➡ Find out the cheapest prices that Fred could pay for these items. How much is his weekly expenditure on food? What other essential food items might he have to buy occasionally? (For example, salt, flour, etc.) What meals can Fred make out of his list of ingredients?

### Coping with bills

Some people find it easier to pay for things like the television, electricity, and gas as they use them, by putting money in a meter. Sometimes you can arrange to pay monthly, and for some bills, such as the telephone and the television licence, you can buy stamps to spread the cost. The alternative is to pay the bills quarterly (once every three months), when they tend to be large, and sometimes all come at once.

If you're not at home when the meter reader calls, you will be sent an estimate of how much to pay. Sometimes, the estimate is very much more than you really owe, as Marie found out:

> I looked at the card they put through my door, with the estimate on it. They said the meter read 44381. I looked at the meter and discovered it said 42411. So they had overestimated by 1970 units. Fortunately, you can ring the Electricity Board and either give them your own reading, or ask them to come out again. They accepted my reading.

If Marie had received a bill which charged her for 1970 units at 5p a unit, how much money would she have been overcharged?

When Marie rang the meter reading section of the Electricity Board, how do you think she explained what she wanted? Practise saying Marie's opening lines with a friend.

# Money at work

> I thought I'd be really well off when I started work. I'd never had so much money before. But I found it a bit of a shock.
>
> First of all I was put on an emergency tax code, so I was paying a lot of tax — though you do get that back in the end.
>
> Then there were all these things that I hadn't counted on having to buy.

What do you think Reena had to spend money on when she started working?

In most jobs, you have to work a 'week in hand'. This means that you won't get paid until the end of the second week after you started work. If you have been on Supplementary Benefit, you can claim money for this period, by using form A7. You may also get a single payment for clothing or equipment needed for work, and fares for your first fifteen days' travel to work.
Ask at or phone your local Social Security office about this.

## How are you paid?

I'm paid weekly, in cash. It comes in a sealed envelope. I have to check the amount is right straight away, and report anything I think is wrong.

I'm paid by cheque. They hand them out on the last Friday of the month. I've got a bank account, so I put it in there. If I didn't have a bank account, I could cash the cheque straight away at a bank where the firm's got an arrangement. But I think it's better not to have all that cash lying around.

My firm pays by credit transfer. That means they pay the cheque straight into your bank account. So when I started there, I had to open an account, and tell the wages clerk my bank and account number.

## Who earns most?

A wage is paid weekly or fortnightly, and a salary is paid monthly. Look at these groups of young people, and see if you can work out who is earning most.

**Group A**
Don is paid £67 per week.
Ella is paid £270 per month.
Danny is paid £3437 per annum (that is, a year).

**Group B**
Colin is paid £52 per week.
Elvis is paid £221 per month.
Dawn is paid £2255 per annum.

**Group C**
Eddie is paid £65 per week.
Cheryl is paid £240 per month.
Sharon is paid £2900 per annum.

## Calculating gross pay from hourly rates

These are the hours worked in one week by some employees at a laundry. Calculate how much their gross pay should be (that is, what they earned before any deductions such as tax and insurance were made).
**1** 36 hours at £2.38 per hour
**2** 36 hours at £2.46 per hour
**3** 38 hours at £2.46 per hour
**4** 40 hours at £2.52 per hour
**5** 40 hours at £2.78 per hour

## Overtime

At the laundry, overtime is paid at the rate of time-and-a-half, so someone who normally earns £2.38 per hour would be paid £2.38 plus £1.19 per hour for overtime work. The overtime rate would therefore be £3.57.

Work out the overtime rate at time-and-a-half for each of the hourly rates given above. If each worker did six hours overtime, how much more money would they get in their gross pay?

## The pay slip

Whether you are paid weekly or monthly, you will get a pay slip with details of your earnings and deductions on it. Here are some of the words used:

**Basic wage:** your wage before any additions or deductions are made.

**Basic rate:** the hourly rate at which you are paid. If you multiply your basic rate by the number of hours you work before overtime, you'll find out what your basic wage is.

**Overtime:** extra hours you work.

**Overtime rate:** the rate at which you are paid for your extra work. It might be time-and-a-half, or double time for Sundays and Bank Holidays.

**Bonus payments:** extra money paid for working well or achieving targets.

**Gross pay:** what you earned, including all overtime and bonus payments, before any deductions were made.

| Payslip |
|---|
| Name |
| Works No |
| Hourly rate |
| Basic wage |
| Overtime |
| Bonus |
| PAYE |
| Nat. Ins. |
| |
| Gross pay |
| **Deductions** |
| Net pay |
| |

**Net pay or 'take-home pay':** what you are left with when all deductions have been made.

## Income tax

Income tax is deducted from your gross pay. It is taken by the Government to help pay for things like schools, hospitals, and defence. Here are some words to do with tax:

**Personal allowance:** the amount you are allowed to earn before you start paying tax. For example, if the personal allowance is £1600, you will not be taxed on the first £1600 which you earn in a year.

**Tax code:** this is worked out for each person, and tells the wages clerk how much tax to deduct.

**Tax return:** the form you fill in to let the Inland Revenue know about your earnings and anything they should take into account when working out your tax code. You should fill one in when you start work, otherwise you'll probably pay too much tax.

**Emergency tax:** if your employer doesn't know how much tax to take from you when you start work, he will put you on emergency tax. This will probably mean that you are paying too much tax.

**Tax rebate:** money given back to you if too much has been deducted in tax.

**PAYE:** stands for 'Pay As You Earn'; most people pay tax in this way.

**P60:** a form which you get every year saying how much tax you have paid in the previous year. It is important. Keep it safe.

**P45:** a form which your employer gives you when you leave his employment, saying how much tax you paid while you were working for him. You must give it to your next employer, so he can work out how much tax to take.

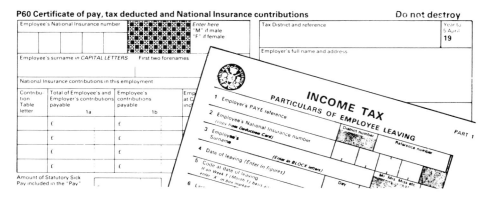

## Filling in a tax return

You must fill in the relevant bits of the form, and sign the Declaration at the end that what you have written is correct, as far as you know. You are supposed to send the form back within thirty days. The parts of the form you are likely to have to fill in are shown opposite. The information which you provide refers to the previous year; so a tax return sent to you in April 1987 refers to the money you earned in the year ending April 1987.

There is not much room on the form for all the details you have to put in. If you need to, use a separate piece of paper to complete the details. There are 91 sections to the present tax form, but you need fill in only a small number of them. The most likely ones are:

**1–3** Put in your occupation, your employer's name and address, and your total earnings. You must also enter details of all other earnings, including casual and spare time.
**4–5** Put in the value of any goods or earnings in kind from your employer
**12** Some DHSS benefits arising from unemployment are taxable. Your benefit office will give you details.
**29** Put in the interest only. You don't pay tax anyway on the first £70 interest.
**33** Put here the amount of interest from your building society account.
**56** You can claim for expenses which have arisen because you had to carry out your job; for example, necessary travelling expenses, and tools and equipment which are necessary for your job, if your employer doesn't provide them. You cannot claim for the cost of travel between home and work.

If you have any problems, the tax office will help you fill the form in.

If you have problems with any of these things when you're at work, your local tax office will help you. They publish a useful leaflet called 'Income Tax and School Leavers'. To find the telephone number of your local tax office, look in the phone book under 'Inland Revenue — Taxes, HM Inspector of'.

You should tell the tax office if your circumstances change: that is, if you get married, divorced, take out a mortgage, or start working for yourself instead of an employer. Any of these things will affect the amount of tax you pay.

**See note**

## Income: 6 April 1985 to 5 April 1986

### Employment, etc

**1-3** Earnings (including fees, bonus, commission, tips, etc)

| Occupation and employers name(s) and address(es) | Self £ | Wife £ |
|---|---|---|
| | | |

**4-5** Benefits/expense allowances

| Details | Self £ | Wife £ |
|---|---|---|

**12** Unemployment or Supplementary benefits *enter the full taxable amount*

| | Self £ | Wife £ |
|---|---|---|

### Interest not taxed before receipt

*Enter ALL the interest on each account or holding*

*Enter interest taxed before receipt on page 4*

| | | Self | Wife |
|---|---|---|---|
| National Savings | NSB Ordinary account ▶ | £ | £ |
| **29** | NSB Investment account ▶ | £ | £ |
| | Deposit or Income Bonds ▶ | £ | £ |

### Interest treated as taxed before receipt (Composite Rate Tax)

**33** Interest from UK banks and deposit takers taxed before receipt

| Name of bank or deposit taker | Self £ | Wife £ |
|---|---|---|
| | | |

**33** Interest from UK building societies

| Name of Society | Self £ | Wife £ |
|---|---|---|
| | | |

## Outgoings: 6 April 1985 to 5 April 1986

### Expenses in employment

**56** Details of expenses

| | Self £ | Wife £ |
|---|---|---|

## Declaration

### False statements can result in prosecution

To the best of my knowledge and belief, the particulars given on this form are correct and complete

*A woman should state after her signature whether she is single, married, widowed, separated or divorced*

Signature

Date

If you are making the return as executor, trustee, receiver, factor, etc give the capacity in which you act and for whom the return is made.

Private address
*use CAPITAL letters*

Postcode

Please enter your National Insurance number if it is not already shown on the front of this form

*If there is any other information which you think may affect your income tax liability, please give details here or on a separate piece of paper.*

## What are your taxes used for?

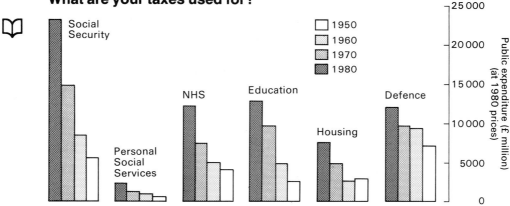

1 What costs most?
2 What costs least?
3 Has expenditure on Social Security payments gone up or down? Why do you think this is?
4 Has expenditure on the National Health Service gone up or down?

## National Insurance contributions

Both you and your employer pay this. Your employer pays more than you do. The money helps to pay for benefits such as:

money if you are sick or have an accident
unemployment benefit
old age pensions
maternity and death grants
child benefit.

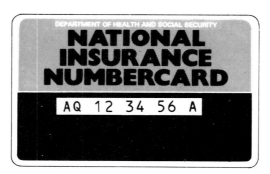

Around the time you leave school, you should be sent a card which shows your National Insurance number. Check it. If any of the facts are wrong, keep a note of the number, but take or send the card to the Social Security office and say what is wrong.

Keep your card in a safe place. Your National Insurance number is used to record your contributions to your National Insurance account. Give your number to your employer whenever you start a new job, otherwise you risk losing benefit if your contributions can't be recorded.

### Sickness

Most employees do not get state sickness benefit for their first eight weeks of sickness in each tax year. Instead, you get statutory sick pay (SSP) from your employer. You need to find out the way your employer handles sick pay.

1 Find out when and how your employer needs to be told you are sick. You may lose SSP if you don't keep to his rules; find out whether your employer wants notice of your sickness in writing, by phone, or both.
2 Find out what evidence of sickness your employer needs. If you are sick for seven days or less, your employer can ask you to fill in a self-certification form supplied by him, or a form supplied by DHSS. If you are sick for seven days or more, your employer can ask you to see your doctor and get a sick note.

## Social Security

In Britain the Social Security system is paid for by National Insurance contributions and taxes.

In return for paying contributions and taxes you get cash help known as 'benefits'. There are three sorts of benefit:

1 **Non-contributory benefit** — for example, child benefit — where you have to meet the conditions which entitle you to the benefit, but you don't have to have paid contributions.
2 **National Insurance benefits** such as unemployment and retirement pensions. You must have paid enough contributions.
3 **Means-tested benefits**, where you don't need to have paid contributions, but you must give details of any money you have coming in. Supplementary benefit is a means-tested benefit.

## Supplementary benefit

If you stay on at school after you are 16 you won't have to pay National Insurance contributions, unless you are doing paid work in your spare time or holidays.

While you are at school you can't get supplementary benefit for yourself unless you are over 16 and
- looking after children of your own, or
- an orphan with no one looking after you, or
- disabled and unlikely to get a job, or
- not living at home and not supported by your parents,

but there are other benefits which you may be entitled to. Some councils make grants to pupils over 16 at school. Ask at your Local Education Authority.

You cannot claim supplementary benefit if:
- you are living with your husband or with a man as his wife
- you have over a certain amount in savings. The DHSS will tell you what the amount is.

If you have just left school or college and have sat your final exams, you claim benefit on the day after you leave school (unless it is a Saturday or Sunday) if you are:
- 19 or over
- looking after children of your own
- an orphan with no one looking after you
- disabled and unlikely to get a job
- not living at home and not supported by your parents.

If you are 16–19, you can claim on the first of these days after you leave school:
- the first Monday in January
- the first Monday after Easter.
- the first Monday in September.

Your parents can go on getting child benefit for you until you can claim supplementary benefit. And if they get unemployment, sickness, or supplementary benefit, they can get extra benefit to help support you.

### How to claim supplementary benefit

If you are under 18, go to the Careers Office. They will give you a card to take to an Unemployment Benefit Office. Take with you your National Insurance number and your school-leaving certificate.

If you are over 18, you can go direct to the Unemployment Benefit Office (UBO). At the UBO you will fill in form B1, which goes to the Social Security office.

If you are entitled to supplementary benefit, the Social Security office will arrange for the UBO to pay it to you. You will have to call at the UBO every fortnight to sign on. The money will come in a Girocheque, which you can pay into a bank account, or cash at a post office.

It's easy to forget how much money actually goes into house furnishings and contents. Insurance companies issue tables like this one to help you calculate the cost of replacing things:

# CONTENTS SUM INSURED CALCULATOR

**Contents:** Your sum insured should be based on what it would cost you to replace all your contents as new with similar items of the same quality. Clothing should be included less an allowance for wear and tear. The check list below is to help you.

### CONTENTS SUM INSURED CHECK LIST (FILL IN TODAY'S VALUE FOR EACH ITEM)

**Kitchen**
Lino tiles _____
Curtains _____
Cooker _____
Refrigerator _____
Washer _____
Vacuum cleaner _____
Iron _____
Ironing board _____
Table _____
Chairs _____
Electric kettle _____
Saucepans _____
Cutlery _____
China & crockery _____
Food _____
Light fitting _____
Radio _____
Freezer _____
Other items _____

**Lounge**
Carpet _____
Curtains _____
3-piece suite _____
Small table _____
T.V.'s etc _____
Light fitting _____
Rug _____
Ornaments, books
pictures _____
Clocks, lamps
and mirrors _____
Other items _____

**Hall/Stairs/Landing**
Carpet _____
Lampshades _____
Mirror _____
Curtains _____
Ornaments and
Pictures _____

Other items _____
**Dining Room**
Carpet _____
Curtain _____
Table _____
Chairs _____
Sideboard _____
Lampshade _____
China, Glass
and Silverware _____
Other items _____

**Main Bedroom**
Wardrobe _____
Dressing table _____
Bedside cabinet _____
Beds _____
Carpet _____
Curtains _____
Light fitting _____
Bedside lights _____

Chairs _____
Other items _____
**No. 2 Bedroom**
Wardrobe _____
Dressing table _____
Bed _____
Bedside cabinet _____
Carpet _____
Curtains _____
Light fitting _____
Other items _____

**No. 3 Bedroom**
Wardrobe _____
Dressing table _____
Bed _____
Bedside cabinet _____
Carpet _____
Curtains _____
Light fitting _____
Other items. _____

**Other rooms**
including loft _____

**Bathroom**
Cabinet _____
Scales _____
Curtains _____
Carpet tiles _____
Bath set _____
Other items _____

**Garage/Outbuildings**
Garden tools _____
D.I.Y. tools _____
Cycles _____
Garden furniture _____
Other items _____

**Miscellaneous**
Clothes (adults)
and children _____

Toys/sports
equipment _____
Personal effects
e.g. transistor
radio, camera,
binoculars etc _____
Jewellery,
watches etc _____
Money _____
Documents _____

**MAIN BEDROOM** _____
**No. 2 BEDROOM** _____
**No. 3 BEDROOM** _____
**OTHER ROOMS** _____
**KITCHEN** _____
**BATHROOM** _____
**GARAGE**
**MISCELLANEOUS** _____
**TOTAL** _____

⟫ Take one or two rooms and write down the amount it would cost to replace all the items on the list at today's prices.

## Insurance for mopeds and motorbikes

It is illegal to ride a moped or a motorbike on a public highway without insurance. Mopeds, which are machines of 50cc or under, are comparatively cheap and simple to insure. A motorbike is slightly more complicated. Here is a sample proposal form. You can pick them up from an insurance broker and practise filling one in.

**Motor Cycle** proposal
Please complete in BLOCK CAPITALS throughout

Town _____

Proposer's full
name starting
with Mr, Mrs,
Miss or other title _____

Address of
Proposer _____

Postcode _____    Age of Proposer _____

Business/
Occupation _____

| | Make and Model | Cubic Capacity | Year of Manufacture | Estimated present value including sidecar | Registration Mark | Price paid | Date of purchase |
|---|---|---|---|---|---|---|---|
| Vehicle to be insured | | | | | | £ | |

Has the vehicle been modified, altered or adapted or been fitted with any additional equipment to give increased performance above the maker's standards?    If so, give details ▶ _____

**1** COVER REQUIRED
Insert in box: **C** for Comprehensive; **F** for Third Party Fire and Theft ▶ _____

**2** Does the motor cycle belong to you?
(Acquiring by Hire Purchase is ownership for the purpose of this question)    If 'NO', state name and address of owner.
Insert YES or NO ▶ _____

**3** Is the motor cycle a moped? ie
(a) If first registered on or before 31st July, 1977 a motor cycle with an engine

### The three types of motor insurance

There are three types of motor insurance, which offer varying degrees of cover. They are:

### 1  Third Party

This cover is required by law. If you do not have it, you are liable to prosecution. Apart from being illegal, if you don't have this cover, you may get involved in serious difficulties if you had an accident in which another person and/or their property were hurt, and it was your fault.

Third Party cover means that if you are involved in an accident in which people or property are damaged through your fault, the insurance company will pay whatever damages or compensation arise. Without this cover, both you and the injured party could suffer; a claim for damages or compensation could be brought against you which could be very large in the case of death or serious injury. You would perhaps never be able to pay it; the injured person or their dependents would perhaps never receive the compensation to which they were entitled. Third Party does not cover any damage to you or your own vehicle. If you borrow or lend a vehicle, it is essential to check that you or your vehicle are covered. You may not be.

### 2  Third Party, Fire, and Theft

This provides Third Party cover, plus cover if your vehicle is damaged or lost through fire or theft.

### 3  Comprehensive

This provides Third Party cover, plus Fire and Theft, plus cover for your own vehicle if it is damaged in an accident, even if you caused it. It is usually much more expensive.

### Some insurance questions to think about

Some insurance cover — such as that for drivers and motorbike or moped riders — is required by law. Some insurance has to be taken out as part of a contract — when buying a house, for example. For the rest it's mostly a question of whether you think it's worth it.

Here are some different views on insurance. Which, if any, do you agree with?

92

# Inflation

Inflation is a general rise in prices, measured over a period of time — usually a year. Inflation is measured in percentages, so we talk of a rise in inflation of, for example, 4%, 6%, or 10%. If there has been a 4% rise in prices in a year, it means that something which cost £1 a year ago now costs £1.04. Can you work out how much more these things will cost if there is inflation at 5%?

|  | Last year | This year |
|---|---|---|
| Washing machine | £300 | |
| Week's groceries | £ 40 | ? |
| Stereo | £350 | |

The major result of inflation is that you can buy less with the same money. This is why people are concerned about wage settlements. On the whole, people expect their standard of living to go up during their working life. If their pay settlements only keep pace with inflation, their standard of living will not increase, since they will only be able to buy the same amount this year as they did last.

**?** Look at these pay settlements, and say whether the workers are better off, worse off, or about the same.

1 Inflation is running at 4%. A group of workers is offered a pay rise of 3%.
2 Inflation is running at 7%. A group of workers is offered a pay rise of 7%.
3 Inflation is running at 6%. A group of workers is offered a pay rise of 8%.

When people say that the rate of inflation has fallen from 6% to 5%, does the fact that the rate has fallen mean:
- there is now no inflation?
- things will cost less than last year?
- things will cost more than last year?

You can no doubt remember some things costing less than they do now; records, clothes, sweets, and food, for example. But when you hear people saying 'I can remember when a pint of milk cost 9d', they often forget that what they were earning then was much less than they are earning now.

**?** Here are some things people say about inflation. Say whether you agree or disagree with them. Are any of the statements actually false?

### Index linking

Some things such as savings or investments are index linked. This means that their value increases with inflation. At the end of this period of saving or investment, it means that you will get back at least what you put in, with some supplementary interest too. It's a good way of making sure that your money doesn't lose its value.

# -4 Working

## Getting ready for work

Most people want a job. For them, work is an important part of their lives. There are many reasons for this, some of which we look at below. One strong reason why people work is because they feel they ought to; that it's wrong to sit around and do nothing. And despite rising unemployment in this country, people find it difficult to accept that they may not always have jobs. This valuing of work for its own sake, rather than for the rewards, such as money, which it brings, is often referred to as the '**work ethic**'.

**?** What ideas do you already have about work? See if you agree or disagree with these statements:
1 Work will be an important part of my life.
2 I shan't mind too much if I can't get a job. There are plenty of other things I'm interested in.
3 Having a job gives you self-respect.
4 It doesn't matter what job you do, so long as you're in work.
5 Work will be more boring than school.
6 People tell you what to do more at work than at school.
7 If you're a girl, it doesn't matter so much what job you do, or if you can't get a job, because you'll probably marry or have kids anyway.
8 I hope to do the same job for the rest of my working life.
9 For most people, work is something they have to put up with so they can enjoy themselves in their free time.

**»** If you asked your parents to say whether they agreed or disagreed with the statements, what would they say?

**?** What impression of work do you get from older workers whom you know?

These are some reasons people give for working:

> I need the money.
> It gives you something to do.
> I'd be bored otherwise.
> It's a way of meeting people.
> It gets you out of the house.
> I enjoy what I do.
> I want to follow a career in this field.
> People look up to you if you've got a job.
> People think you're nothing if you haven't got a job.
> My parents say I must get a job.
> I can't afford not to work.

**▶** 1 Which of the reasons are to do with earning money?
2 Which reasons are to do with enjoying the job for itself?
3 Which reasons are to do with what other people think about the person?
4 Which reasons are to do with what the person thinks about him- or herself?

Can you add any more reasons for working to the list?

Here are some reasons people give for not working:

> There aren't any jobs around here.
> The jobs I've been offered are rubbish.
> I don't particularly want to work. I'd rather go fishing.
> Work is boring.

Can you think of any more?
On the whole, do you think that there are more reasons for working or for not working?

**▦** Interview some people who are in jobs at the moment. Ask them what the most important thing about work is to them. Things like:
- the actual job they do
- whether they meet people or not
- having friends at work
- feeling they're doing something useful.

How would they feel if they lost their job suddenly? What difference would it make to their lives?

## Making the most of yourself

If you're looking for work, you may have a lot of skills and experiences already which will be useful to you in work, and which an employer will value. These skills and experiences may not have been directly connected with paid employment or work experience, but are the sort of things people need to be able to have or to do in order to get on at work. Look at these lists

**?** of things which young people have done in their spare time. What things might they have done or learnt that would be useful to them in the future?

> baby-sitting
> early morning paper round
> helping in an old people's home
> collecting for charity
> playing for a sports team
> helping at a playgroup
> helping to put a community magazine together

▶ Make a list of all the things you have done, whether they were paid jobs or not, that might increase your chances of finding and keeping a job.

**?** ## What skills do you think employers are looking for?

Employers have to teach new employees how to do the job anyway — they probably won't expect you to know all that much about it. So what skills or qualities do they think are important? If you were an employer, how would you rate the importance of the following skills?

1 Is able to understand what's being said.
2 Is able to do as he/she is told.
3 Is able to remember instructions.
4 Is friendly and has a co-operative attitude.
5 Gets on well with people.
6 Is adaptable and fits in.
7 Is honest.
8 Is chatty and sympathetic.
9 Can solve his/her own problems.
10 Sees a job through properly.
11 Concentrates and doesn't let attention wander.
12 Does things on his/her own.
13 Is reliable and a good timekeeper.
14 Never takes time off unnecessarily.

Work experience doesn't train you for the job; you couldn't say you were qualified to do the job after just a few weeks on a scheme. But it does give you a lot of advantages and the opportunity to find out what work is like.

▶ What things do you think work experience gives you? Write them down.

# Choosing a job

▶ Write down the answers to these questions:

1 What are you going to do at the end of this year? Give your reasons for this choice.
2 How did you find out about it?
3 Who have you discussed your choice with?
4 What have they said?
5 Have you considered anything else?

## National and local job markets

How much do you know about the job scene in this country, and in your local area? Say whether you think that these industries and jobs are expanding or declining **a** in Britain as a whole, and **b** in your area:

catering

hotel work

ship building

mining

clerical work

computing

shops and retailing

insurance, banking, and finance

leisure industries

manufacturing

entertainment

If you don't know the answer, ask your careers teacher.

In the country as a whole, the manufacturing industries are increasing their productivity. But the increased productivity is due to the greater use of machines, robots, and microprocessors. What effect does this have on jobs?

If manufacturers are making more money from their increased productivity, do you think they will spend the money on jobs or new machines?

If technology is described as 'labour saving', do you think this means jobs are created, or jobs are lost?

Some people believe that new jobs will be created in the service industries as those with more money and leisure look for ways of spending them. What are the service industries? Name as many as you can.

## Unskilled and skilled work

**Unskilled workers** are those without any special training. Many unskilled jobs are physically hard and demand strength. They may be repetitive. The rates of pay vary a great deal. If the work is very unpleasant, the rate of pay can be high. On the whole, there is little chance of promotion. There is often the chance of overtime.

**Skilled workers** have trained for their jobs. They may have gone to a College of Further Education, been apprenticed, or been trained by the firm. During training, they don't earn much. But after they are trained, they will generally be on a higher rate of pay than the unskilled worker. They have the chance of promotion.

Are you most likely to get the following in a skilled or an unskilled job?

high wages while the work is there

job security

salary

pension

plenty of chance for overtime

promotion up a career structure

training opportunities

seasonal work

availability of work affected by weather

paid holidays

perks (can you give examples of perks in jobs?)

What about jobs in your area? What sort of jobs do people do in the area where you live?

Look at job advertisements in the local paper. Try to divide them up into the following categories:

>
office
manual/manufacturing
social/helping
medical/hospital
hotel/catering
retail/sales
scientific/laboratory
design
literary/creative

1 Into which categories do most job vacancies fall?
2 What sort of jobs would you apply for? Why?
3 What jobs would you not do? Why?
4 How much chance do you think you've got of getting the job you want?
5 What are the things in your favour?
6 What are the things against you?
7 What can you do to improve your chances, apart from trying to get more or better exam passes?

List now ten things which you consider to be your strengths.
Think of as many jobs as you can where these strengths would be helpful to you. Here are Krishna's ten points:

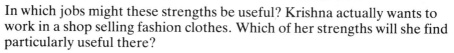

1 I'm good with people.
2 I can get to places on time.
3 I'm not easily upset.
4 I'm quite calm in difficult situations.
5 I like meeting people and talking to them.
6 I like writing.
7 I don't mind doing what I'm told.
8 I'm physically quite strong and healthy.
9 I'm honest.
10 I don't mind repetitive jobs.

In which jobs might these strengths be useful? Krishna actually wants to work in a shop selling fashion clothes. Which of her strengths will she find particularly useful there?

Most people have a dream job which they would like to do. Say what yours is, and what your reasons for doing it would be. What are the things that you think go with your dream job; e.g. travel, fame, money, admiration?

Ask older workers whom you know if they had a dream about what job they would have liked to do when they were younger. Ask them what the job would have been, and why they wanted to do it. Ask them if they were disappointed in the job(s) that they did get.

# Ways of applying for jobs

## Formal ways of getting a job

### 1 Using the Careers Office

During your last year at school, you will meet the Careers Officer, who will ask you questions and get to know the sort of person you are, and what sort of jobs would suit you.

What sort of questions might the Careers Officer ask in order to find out about you and what sort of jobs you're interested in? Which of these questions might he or she ask?

'What television programmes did you watch last night?'
'What are your hobbies and interests?'
'Where are you going for your holidays this year?'
'Have you any work experience?'
'Have you ever done any community or voluntary work?'
'What are your favourite pop groups?'
'Are you sitting any examinations?'

What answers would you give to the questions you think you might be asked?
Get a friend to ask you them, and practise answering.

### How the Careers Office works

When an employer has a vacancy for a young person, he or she tells the Careers Office the following things:

what the job is
what the young person will be expected to do in the job
whether there's any training
what the hours are
what the pay is
what the holidays are
what the prospects are for the young worker in the firm.

If the Careers Officer thinks the vacancy will interest you, he or she will make an appointment for you to see the employer. The Careers Officer will give you an introduction card to take with you.

## 2　The Jobcentre

This is more suitable for slightly older school leavers. The difference at the Jobcentre is that there is no-one there who has kept in touch with you and what you're looking for since your last year at school.

Cards with details of vacancies are on display under headings like 'clerical', 'hotel', 'building'. If you see a job you like, you write down the reference number and take it to the person at the desk.

You will be told more about the job and an interview may be arranged for you. So if you go to the Jobcentre, be prepared to go for an interview that day; this means dressing appropriately and taking anything you might need with you.

## 3　Employment Agencies

Most big towns have Employment Agencies. You can register with them by calling in or by phoning them up. They are listed in Yellow Pages under 'Employment Agencies'. It doesn't cost you anything to register, since the employer pays the fees.

A lot of agencies offer part-time or temporary employment, where the employment conditions may not be so good. You may not get holiday pay or sick pay, for example.

## 4　Vacancy Boards in shops or outside firms and factories

A firm may advertise in its own window or at the factory gate. These vacancies are likely to go quickly.

❓ How would you go about enquiring after a vacancy advertised
**a** in a newsagent's window?
**b** at a factory gate?
☺ What would you ask first?

101

## 5    The Situations Vacant column in your local newspaper

Here you will usually find jobs advertised under headings. Some of these jobs may be suitable for school leavers. Buy a newspaper regularly, and see what sort of jobs are advertised. If you're serious about job hunting, you'll have to get the paper as soon as it comes out. A delay of even a few hours may mean you miss the vacancy.

1  From the Situations Vacant column in your local paper, how many employers ask you to write to them to apply for the job?
2  How many ask you to ring for an application form?
3  How many ask you to ring for an appointment?

Think about how you would tackle an employer advertising in the local paper. If you feel nervous about writing or phoning, have a look at the sections in **Communicating** on pages 49–62.

### 6    Trade journals

These are kept in your local library. Have a look through the journal which is concerned with the sort of work you're interested in. Make a note of any employers who are in your area, and whom you could contact. (See 'Contacting employers', below.)

## Informal ways of getting a job

### 1    Contacts

A lot of young people still get jobs because they know someone who works in the firm, who has recommended them, or who knows there's a vacancy which might be suitable. Ask parents, other relatives, and friends to tell you if they hear of any jobs available.

If your dad came home from work one day and said there was a vacancy for a young person where he worked, how would you go about applying for the job? Which of these ways would you use?

1  Ask your dad to make an appointment for you with the right person.
2  Ask your dad the name of the person to go to so that you could make an appointment.
3  Phone up the firm, explain who you are, and ask for further information about the job.
4  Ask your dad to apply on your behalf.

With a friend, practise saying things like:
'I understand you have a vacancy for a school leaver.'
'Can you give me some more details about the vacancy?'

## 2   Contacting employers

It's worth getting yourself known by local employers, without making a nuisance of yourself. You can introduce yourself by:

1 phoning and asking to speak to the Personnel Manager, explaining that you are looking for work, and asking them to consider you if a vacancy arises; or
2 writing to the Personnel Manager, with details of yourself, your interests, qualifications, and the sort of job you're looking for, together with reasons why the job interests you.

The advantages are that the firm may put you on their books and let you know of any vacancies that arise; they may be impressed by your keenness.

The disadvantages are that you might simply be ignored, or they might be unhelpful. It's up to you to decide whether the advantages outweigh the risks.

Good sources of employers to try are:
      Yellow Pages
      trade journals
      Situations Vacant columns.

### Further work

Name all the ways you now know of finding a job. For each one, say what you think the advantages and disadvantages of the method are. Which method do you think will suit you best?

Ask people you know who are in work how they got their jobs. How many jobs were got through formal methods, and how many through informal methods?

### The jobsearch game

The class divides into groups of five. Each group represents a local employer, which decides what its business is and what vacancies it has, and draws up an advertisement for each vacancy. The advertisements are stuck on the wall where everyone can see them. Make sure the advertisement says clearly what the job is, how candidates should make their application (in person, in writing, or by phone), and to whom the application should be addressed.

As well as belonging to an employer group, each member of the class must decide on one or more vacancies for which he or she is going to apply, and must make the appropriate application.

The employer groups call suitable candidates and interview them. They decide which person they would like to employ, and offer him or her the job.

At the end of the game, answer the following questions:

*When you were in an employer group:*

1 How did you decide what questions to ask at the interview?
2 How did you decide on the best candidate?
3 How did the applicants do at interview? What answers impressed you?
4 What sort of answers made a bad impression?
5 Have you now got any advice for people when they go for job interviews?

*When you were being interviewed:*
1 What was the worst thing?
2 Were you surprised at any of the questions?
3 How do you think you did?
4 Have you learnt anything useful from this exercise? If so, what?

# Fitting in at work

Things are different at work. This section is to help you think about some of the ways in which work is different.

Look at this list. Decide in each case how things are at the moment, at school, and how you think they'll be at work.

1 How long is your working day?
2 How long do you spend travelling?
3 What time do you get up?
4 Can you wear what you like?
5 Are you free to decide what to do each day?
6 Do you have choice in what you do each day?
7 Is there variety in what you do each day?
8 How long do you spend on each task?
9 How fast do you have to work?
10 Does your performance affect anyone else?
11 Do you have to work as part of a team?
12 Do you have to get things right first time?
13 Does it matter if you listen or not?
14 Do you have money?
15 Do you have status?
16 Do you have responsibility?

There may not be any right or wrong answers to the list; it's just your opinion that matters. When you've finished, compare your answers with a friend's. Do you agree in your opinions? If not, try to explain your arguments to each other.

Here are some young people's comments on what surprised them about work.

➡️ Make a list of all the problems and surprises these young people met at work. Did they all solve their problems? Do you think they chose the best solutions? Would you have done anything different?

❓ Some people have not yet solved their problems. What advice would you give them?

Here are some remarks employers and supervisors made about young people:

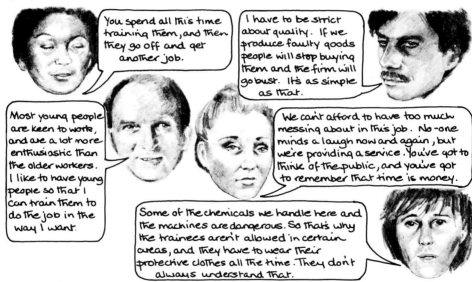

✋ Imagine an encounter between one of these supervisors, and one of the young people who had described their first days at work. Either role-play or write out the conversation that they have, as they each try to explain their point of view.

❓ What worries you about starting work?
What things to do with starting work do you feel confident about?
What suggestions do you have for someone who is starting work and wants to give a good impression?

➡️ Draw a cartoon or write a story about your first days at work, in which the worst things you can imagine happen to you. Now think about how you could prevent them happening, or what you would do if they did happen.

What are the options for young people who think they've got problems at work? Walking out may seem the easiest solution, and may make you feel better; but it doesn't really solve anything, and you lose your job as well.

**?** What would you do if the following things happened?

1 Someone mentioned training courses when you were interviewed. But since you've started work, no-one's said anything more about them. You'd like to find out what training is available to you.

2 You've been in this job six months. Although you didn't mind it at first, they still expect you to do the clearing up at the end of the day. Sometimes it means you leave later than everyone else, and you don't get any extra pay.

3 Your pay is less than usual this week.

4 Although you've been in the job longer, new people keep getting promoted above you. You think it's because you're black.

5 It's against company rules to take stuff from the stores without having it signed out first. You know some of your mates take stuff without authorization. You suspect that they're nicking it to sell outside work.

In some of these situations, you may have opted to do nothing. But where you decide to speak to the person who is concerned, or to someone whom you think can help you with the problem, what would you actually say to describe what is worrying you? Try practising with a friend.

# Training

## At school

In order to prepare their pupils for life after school, more and more schools are including a technical or vocational element in what they teach.

Because not everyone will find it easy to get a job when they leave school, some people say that it's better to give young people a range of skills which will be useful to them in a variety of jobs. They are called 'transferable' skills, because you can transfer them from one job to another.

**?** Which of these skills do you think could be called transferable, and would be useful in a number of jobs?

neat handwriting
good with figures
able to use a number of tools
able to use telephone
able to use typewriter or computer keyboard
able to change points and plugs
able to measure and calculate area
able to use a lathe
able to use weighing scales
able to use a till
able to get on with people
able to follow instructions
able to complete a task in a given time

For each skill that you think is 'transferable', can you think of three or four jobs where it would be useful?

What other skills are you learning at school that are not on this list?
Can you say which of them you think are transferable?
Is school training you in any other way?
Are there other ways in which you think school could train you? What are they?

## At work

An employer is not legally obliged to train you. The training you receive will vary from job to job, from workplace to workplace, and from industry to industry. It may take place on the job, at certain times each week;

or off the job, in a college or residential centre.
Here are some terms which are to do with training, and their explanations:

**Induction course:** most firms, particularly large ones who take on a lot of new people at a time, run courses for people who are just starting to work for them. The course is to introduce you to the company, what it does, how it operates, what health and safety rules you have to observe, who to go to if you've got an enquiry or a complaint, and so on.

If it were your first day at work, what would you like to be told about the place you had just joined?

How would you organize an induction course for someone who had just joined your school?

**Day release:** means that the employer allows you to attend college for one day a week without loss of basic pay.

**Block release:** means that the employer allows you to attend college for a full time period of up to twelve months.

Both day release and block release courses are run by colleges in association with local industry.

# Unions

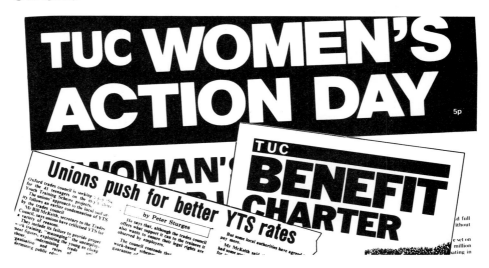

What do you know about trade unions? What are your impressions of them? To find out, see if you agree or disagree with the following statements:

1 The unions have harmed the economy of this country.
2 The unions have made great improvements in the living standards and working conditions of their members.
3 Unions are responsible for disputes and poor relations with employers.
4 The only thing that unions are interested in is going on strike.
5 Unions don't do anything for young people.
6 The main thing you hear in the news is about unions striking over pay, but in fact they do a lot more for their members than argue about better pay.
7 If you've got a problem at work, your union will help you sort it out.
8 It's only fair that people should join their union, since if the union gets better working conditions, everyone benefits.

Now think where you've got your information about trade unions from: other workers? your parents? the television and newspapers?
Which of the statements about unions do you think your parents would agree or disagree with?
On the whole, do your parents regard unions as a good thing?
On the whole, do you think the press and television present unions as a good thing?
If you were in work, would you join a union or not?

Finish this statement, and then go on to read about unions.
I think that the main purpose of a union is . . .

## What is a trade union?

A trade union is a group of working people who have joined together to talk to employers about pay and conditions at work, instead of each member talking to the employer individually. Employers generally prefer to negotiate with the union rather than with individuals.

The purposes of a trade union are:
- to help with better pay
- to help you if you are sacked unfairly
- to help you if you are made redundant
- to make sure you get proper training
- to fight for you if you are discriminated against at work because of your race, colour or sex
- to help get better and safer conditions for people to work in.

In addition, many unions provide services for their members, such as:
> insurance
> legal advice and help
> cheap holidays
> discount schemes
> medical treatment
> educational courses.

### How do you join?

In some jobs, you can choose whether you join a union. In other jobs, it is compulsory. A workplace where it is compulsory to join a union is called a **closed shop**.

If you join a union, you will have to pay a weekly or monthly sum of money to the union's funds. For young people, this will only mean a small sum each week. Most unions pay a contribution to the Labour party; this is called the 'political levy'. You can choose to opt out of this.

When you start work, the Shop Steward will probably come and ask you if you want to join the union. The Shop Steward is the person who represents the workers in a particular workplace. He or she is sometimes called the Union Representative. He or she speaks on your behalf to management and employers, and helps organize union meetings in the workplace. The steward is not paid for his or her union work, though some firms allow time for union duties.

If no-one asks you and you do want to join the union or find out more, ask the people you work with who the Shop Steward is.

### What do you have to do once you're a member?

It's a good idea to go to meetings to find out what is happening. Look for the union notice-board that tells you when and where the meeting will take place. At the meetings, you will be able to discuss and vote on what the union does. The union follows the wishes of the majority.

Some meetings may be held in working hours, in which case you should be allowed time off to attend. Other meetings may be held outside working hours — in meal breaks, or after work.

### Terms

Here are some more terms which people use when talking about unions:

**Collective bargaining** is when the union and the employer meet to talk about some issue such as pay or conditions of work. Each side puts its argument. Usually a compromise which is acceptable to both sides is reached.

A **strike** may occur when discussions and negotiations have broken down. The union calls upon its members to stop work. The **official strike** is the strongest action that a union can take.

An **unofficial strike** occurs when workers strike without the support of their union.

During a strike, **pickets** are workers who try to inform other workers about the dispute and persuade them not to break the strike.

**Arbitration** occurs when an employer and union who cannot agree call in a third person to make a decision.

**?** Can you explain to someone who has just started work what the following terms mean?

      a closed shop
      a shop steward
      collective bargaining
      union dues
      redundancy
      training
      a strike
      working conditions

## If you can't get a job

### Consider the choices

What can you do if there's not a job for you to go to? There are various reasons why unemployment among young people is high, and likely to remain so. Fortunately, few people now think that it's the fault of young people themselves if they can't find work.

    If you can't get a job, there are a number of choices open to you; this diagram represents one person's thinking about the choices open to her.
Try doing one for yourself.

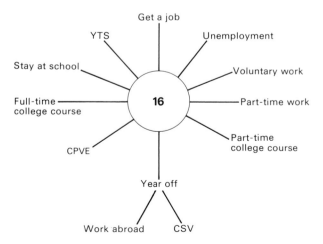

You'll need to ask yourself some of these questions:

1 Could I/would I stay on at school?
2 Would I go to the local Further Education College?
3 Do they run suitable courses?
4 Do I want to study part-time?
5 Would I consider voluntary work?
6 Would I take a job that was not what I really wanted to do, just to keep going?
7 Can I make my own work?
8 Could I eventually become self-employed?
9 What local agencies or drop-in centres are there that could help?
10 Would I consider moving to find work?
11 How can I make the most of having a lot of time available?
12 Can I do a Certificate of Pre Vocational Education (CPVE) in my school or local college?

## Staying on in full-time education

More young people are choosing to do this if they can't get a job straight away. What are the advantages?

- You could try for more or better exam passes. Or if you go to a Further Education College, you may be able to follow courses that aren't on offer at school, but which are more linked to the needs of local industry.
- You can still get careers advice and information from teachers and staff.
- It's a good way of spending time if you are too young for the job or training that you want.

## Voluntary work

You may already have contacts in the community through school Community Service schemes. If not, try your telephone directory for the county 'Council for Voluntary Service'. Look under the name of your county. There may also be entries under 'Voluntary' or 'Volunteer'. Other good people to ask would be your youth club leader or youth worker, or the Citizens' Advice Bureau.

Community Service
    Volunteers
237 Pentonville Road
London N1 9JN
find large numbers of people
voluntary work each year.
Volunteers receive a small weekly
allowance.
The Voluntary Service Opportunity
Register is obtainable from the
        National Youth Bureau,
        17 Albion St
        Leicester.
Send a large stamped addressed
envelope.

What are the advantages?
- It can be a useful and satisfying way of using your time.
- It gives you the chance to give a positive answer to anyone who asks you what you've been doing since leaving school.
- Sometimes the organizations for whom you're doing voluntary work will give you a reference. Again this is useful when you come to job-hunting.
- Doing voluntary work doesn't interfere with your benefit, though you have to make sure that you're available to sign on and to go for job interviews if necessary.

## Moving away for work

This idea won't suit everybody; would it suit you? It's worth considering if:
- you are fairly certain of a job where you're going
- you have got or can find accommodation. You will be worse off if you move from your home area to find work, are unsuccessful, and have nowhere to live either. Both making yourself presentable for employers, and getting benefit, will be more difficult.

## Working for yourself

Is there something which you really love doing, or which you're good at, which could earn you money? If so, you might consider trying to work for yourself. Or a group of you could get together and work as a team making work for yourselves. Whatever you do will need careful planning and organization. Here are some things to think about:

1 How can you find what work might be needed? Look in the small ads in newsagents or post offices and shops, and see what services people seem to be asking for.
2 How will you make yourself known? How will you advertise yourself?
3 How will you decide what to charge?
4 How much money do you need to live off?
5 Do you need any capital (money you've already saved or can borrow) to buy things like tools and equipment, to advertise, or to keep yourself while you get started?

What tools and equipment do you think you'd need to set yourself up in the following jobs?

> gardening
> car washing
> same-day delivery service for your local area
> sewing or knitting
> window cleaning
> domestic/mother's help
> caterer
> freelance typist
> painter/decorator

What are the good things about working for yourself?

You get real satisfaction from doing something you enjoy or are good at, and knowing that it's for yourself. There's not someone telling you what to do. The harder you work, the more you earn; but for me the money's not everything, so long as I get enough to live on.

What are the things to look out for if you're working for yourself?

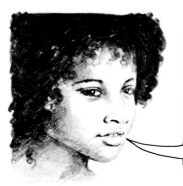

You've got to be better at the job than if you were working for someone else, because your reputation depends on it. Word soon gets around if you do a bad job.

You've got to keep accounts and books straight. I keep all the bills I get, and have copies of bills I send out.
Then you have to keep your own tax and National Insurance contributions sorted out. If you worked for someone else, he or she would arrange it.

### The Youth Training Scheme

If you cannot get a job, you will be offered a place on the Youth Training Scheme.

### What is it?

The Youth Training Scheme, which was launched in 1983, has been expanded and developed to give 16-year-old school leavers two years of training, and 17-year-old school leavers one year, with special arrangements for disabled young people and some other groups.

You will get:

- at least 20 weeks training off-the-job in a college or training centre
- on-the-job training
- planned work experience
- in the second year, specific skill training leading to vocational qualifications
- a tax-free allowance of £27.30 a week in your first year, increasing to £35 in your second year (1986 rates). You won't have to pay National Insurance contributions, and you get paid holiday. You may get help with travel costs.

It's important to find out what sorts of schemes are operating in your area, and which would suit you. Find out from your Careers Office. Ask people who've been on it what they thought of it, and how you can make the most of your time on YTS. What did people do after YTS?

## Structuring a day without work

What are the worst things about being without work? Here are one person's comments:

At first it was quite nice in the summer. You can go out, I spent a lot of time fishing, and there were always my mates to go and see.

Gradually things changed; I got more and more bored, and felt less able to decide what to do each day. Even the trip to the Jobcentre or to sign on became a big effort. I saw less of my mates and spent more time at home just doing nothing. I'd wake up late, spend half the day in bed, just to kill time. I annoyed my Mum because I just hung around, and I got very depressed and alone. I suppose it got to the stage where I just gave up looking for work.

What are Joe's feelings about being out of work? Even if the job prospects were very gloomy, there were things Joe could have done, rather than stay in bed and get depressed.

Beverley goes to a drop-in centre for unemployed young people:

I was just beginning to feel no good as a person, when I saw this article in the free paper about a drop-in centre.

There are lots of good things about it. There are other people there, for a start, who are in the same position as you are, and who don't make you feel you're the only person in the world who can't get a job. There's music and things like a photographic workshop, and it's good to be able to make things and feel you're using your time constructively.
Going there has given me back some of my self-respect.

Find out if there are any such drop-in centres in your area. Ask them what they've got to offer.

# 5 Politics

## Having a say

We look at making decisions for yourself in Chapter 8. But what about decisions which are made by or for a group? Do you feel, like Jane and Leroy, that you have no say? Or are you happy to let others decide for you?

Let's take a look at how some of the groups you're involved in make decisions, and whether you think they go about things in the right way.

➡ Here are some ways in which decisions might be made. Say which applies in your case. Then finish the sentence after each group.

### 1 Family

**a** In my family, we make decisions jointly, and talk about things till we all agree.
**b** In my family, no one really decides. We just row about things.
**c** Someone else decides, and then tells me what's going to happen. I'm never asked.
**d** We do whatever it is that most people want. We all get our say.

I feel that my family's way of making decisions is . . .

### 2 School

**a** In my school, they let us decide some things, but we don't have any real say. They can always do what they want and ignore what you want.
**b** We help make decisions on some things that matter to us.
**c** I don't think we should be involved in making decisions. After all, it's their job. That's what they're paid for.
**d** There ought to be more chance for us to say what we think.

I feel that the way decisions are made in my school is . . .

### 3 Friends

**a** In my group we do what the leaders decide. They always have good ideas.
**b** In my group we all decide on what to do. We do what the majority wants.
**c** We take it in turns to decide.
**d** We each do what we want.

I feel the way that my group of friends makes decisions is . . .

**?** Look through the ways of making decisions that people used in the groups above. Can you find examples of the following?

- **negotiation**, or a 'give-and-take' attitude
- a **democratic decision**, where the group did what the majority wanted
- **apathy**, where someone didn't join in.

**?** How do you see your involvement in groups? Which of these statements do you agree with?

**1** If you belong to a group, you should contribute to the way it's run.
**2** It's best to let the experts look after things.
**3** I'm not very good at deciding things and telling people what to do.
**4** I'd rather leave it to someone who's good at it.
**5** I'd like to do more, but it takes too much time and I'm very busy already.
**6** I'm happy the way things are.
**7** If there was something I really felt strongly about, I'd make it known then.

The next sections look at the way decisions are made in your local community—the town, city, or county you come from—and how decisions are made in the country as a whole.

## Local government

Some government is carried out from London and is known as **central government**. Some is carried out on a local basis, and is known as **local government**.

### What does local government do?

Local government provides a range of services, often described as being 'from the cradle to the grave', because they care for all aspects of people's welfare, from their birth to their death. The services are:

**1 Protective services**
Local government is responsible for providing:

- local police services
- the fire service
- consumer protection; trading standards officers investigate traders and check on weights and measures and descriptions of goods
- licensing — of premises, services, gun owners, child minders, pawn brokers and money-lenders, for example.

## 2 Environmental services

These aim to improve our environment through:

- Environmental health services such as refuse collection, street cleaning, the provision of public toilets, and making sure that places are not too noisy or smoky from industry.
- Maintaining roads and providing a Road Safety Officer who promotes people's awareness of safe conduct on the roads.
- Planning how land is to be used in the area — whether it is to be used for roads, housing, schools, shops, or industry. The plans must be well publicized, and the public must be allowed to voice any objections. Extensions to houses, unless they are very small, must have planning permission.
- Protecting and conserving woodland, parkland, and buildings of historic interest.
- Providing emergency services in times of war or natural disasters such as flood or heavy snow.

**?** How many things in this picture are provided by local government?

## 3 Personal services

These look after our welfare, and cover:

**Education** The local authorities are responsible for providing, without charge, adequate secondary, primary, and nursery schooling for the ten million school children in Britain. Authorities also provide full- and part-time courses in Colleges of Further Education, adult education classes, and grants for students entering higher education courses.

**Careers advice** The Careers Officer who comes to talk to you, or whom you visit at the Careers Office, is employed by the local authority.

**Personal Social Services** to help the more vulnerable people in our society. Facilities like residential homes, foster care, day-time care, training centres for the handicapped, help in the home, and similar services, are provided by the local authority for those in need.

**Housing**   Local authorities provide about one third of housing in this country, in the form of council housing.

## 4   Amenity services
These include things like playgrounds, parks, museums, libraries, art galleries, sports centres, swimming pools, and so on.

## Local government elections
Local councils are elected for a fixed term of four years. In most local authorities, the councillors are elected all together, every four years.

  Local government elections are usually well publicized, but not many people vote in them. The turn-out is about 40% of people who are entitled to vote, compared to about 70% or 80% in Parliamentary elections (General Elections). Why do you think this is?

## What does a councillor do?
A recent report says that an average councillor spends nearly 80 hours a month on his or her duties. He or she spends this time on:
- attending council and committee meetings
- dealing with electors' problems, such as housing, and holding 'surgeries' where he or she can be reached by anyone who wants to talk to him or her about community matters
- serving as a council nominee on other organizations, such as the health authority
- attending semi-social functions, such as fetes and speech days.

Councillors are not paid, but they can claim an attendance allowance.

  Although there will be variations depending on the type of region a councillor represents, as a national average councillors tend to be:
- older: 50% of councillors are over 54, and less than 10% are under 45
- male: less than one councillor in five is female
- in white-collar jobs.

Why do you think this is?

Find out, if you don't already know, who your local councillors are. Ask if any of them would be prepared to talk to you about their work. You could ask them the following questions:

1 How do you spend your day?
2 What sort of problems do people come to you with?
3 Are you connected with a political party?
4 Does this affect your work at council level?

## Where do local authorities get their money from?

Their money comes from three main sources:
1 From council house rents and fees which they charge for services, such as car parks and bus fares.
2 From grants or subsidies from central government. The biggest grant which central government makes to the local authorities is called the 'rate support grant'.
3 From rates.
   They may also get extra money from things like selling land or council houses.

## What are the rates?

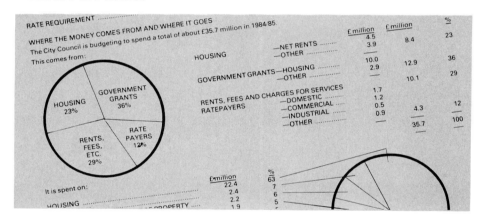

Rates are a form of local property taxation. Generally speaking, the more the property is worth, and the more amenities the council provides in the area, the higher the rate due. The owner (or in some cases the occupier) of the property has to pay the rates due.

 Find out what the rates are on different types of property in your area.

### How does the system work?
Property is given a valuation, based on what the annual rent might be if the property were to be let. This is called the **rateable value**.
   Every year the authority fixes a rate in the pound. The owner or occupier has to pay that amount for every pound of the rateable value of the property. So, if the rate fixed by the authority is 80p in the pound, and the property's rateable value is £200, the rates due are £0.80 × 200 = £160.

### What's all this got to do with me?

In a small group, think of things which the local authority does which might affect you; or things which it doesn't do, about which you feel strongly.

If you can't think of anything, have a look in your local newspaper. Probably a weekly one is best. Can you find any articles on people's reactions to what the council says it is going to do about:

- schools
- roads
- playgrounds and other facilities
- tourism
- industrial or commercial development?

Are there any stories about people going to their councillors to ask them for support in something about which they feel strongly?

Do you know anyone who has bothered to
- go to a public meeting, *or*
- sign a petition, *or*
- write to the local paper, *or*
- contact their councillor

about something? Ask them whether it did any good. Were they happy with the response they got?

Is there anything about which *you* feel strongly enough to lobby your councillor?

# National politics

The politics of the country and the goings-on of the various political parties may seem more remote to you than what goes on at the local level. Or do you feel that you are more in touch with national politics because of news in papers, and on television and radio?

Try answering these questions:

1 Who is Prime Minister at the moment?
2 Which political party is in office?
3 Which political party is in opposition?
4 Who is leader of the opposition party?
5 Can you name any other political parties?
6 What is the name of your MP?
7 Which party does he or she belong to?

## Voting

You are entitled to vote if your name is on the electoral register. You have to be 18 before you can vote in an election. But this doesn't mean that you have to wait till you are 18 to get on the electoral register. If you are 16 or 17, you should be entered on the register, as you may reach the age of 18 during the time it is used for an election.

The electoral registration form is delivered to every household each autumn. The householder has to complete it, but you should make sure that you are included if you think you qualify.

You can check the register, which is on display in town halls, libraries, and main post offices. Go to one of these places and find out if you or members of your family are on the register. If you think you've been left out, you should let the Electoral Registration Officer know.

## What happens in a General Election?

A Government holds office for a maximum period of five years. The Prime Minister decides when the next election will be held within the five year period.

1 What year was the last General Election?
2 If the present Government stays in office for five years, when will the next General Election be?
3 How old will you be then?
4 When should you check that your name is on the Electoral Register?

Find out the dates of all the General Elections held during the last twenty years.

## Constituencies

Great Britain is divided into 650 electoral areas called **constituencies**. Each constituency elects one Member of Parliament to represent approximately 75000 voters.

## Election Day

A few days before the election, every voter receives a polling card telling him or her where to go to vote. Polling stations are usually in schools or libraries or other public places.

Each voter has one vote. The ballot paper gives the name, address, and political party of each candidate in your constituency. You vote by putting a cross against the person you want to represent you in Parliament.

If you are sixteen and have a job, you'll probably pay taxes to the government. But you can't vote till you're 18 and you can't stand for election to Parliament until you're 21.

| | |
|---|---|
| 1 | **BROWN**<br>(JOHN EDWARD Brown, of 52, George Street, Bristol, merchant.) |
| 2 | **BROWN**<br>(THOMAS WILLIAM Brown, of 136, London Road, Swindon, salesman.) |
| 3 | **JONES**<br>(William David Jones, of High Elms, Wilts., gentleman.) |
| 4 | **MERTON**<br>(Hon. George Travis, commonly called Viscount Merton, of Swansworth, Berks.) |
| 5 | **SMITH**<br>(Mary Smith, of 72 High Street, Bath, married woman.) |

1 Do you think the age differences are fair?
2 Should you be able to say how your taxes are to be used at the same time as you have to pay them?
3 Should you be able to stand for elections at the same time as you are able to vote? If so what age should this be?

## What do the parties stand for?

You probably have some ideas about the policies of the main political parties. Write down what you think the Conservative, Labour, and Alliance parties would do in the areas of:

- education
- defence
- jobs and unemployment.
- the National Health Service
- taxes.

Compare your answer with a friend's. Do you agree? If you disagree, how can you find out who is right?

Each party's **manifesto** sets out what the party would do if it were voted into power. But manifestos are usually only issued at election time, and anyway parties are not bound to follow them.

What can you find in the daily papers that tells you what the political parties stand for?

## Trying out the process

You may already run elections in school to choose various officers. You could try running your own mock political election.

### How to go about it

Someone is the Returning Officer. His or her job is to see that everyone else obeys the campaign rules, that the timetable is kept to, and that the votes are counted fairly. He or she should organize one occasion on which all the candidates speak, so that the voters can compare their policies.

Everyone else decides whether they are going to stand for election, help a particular party fight its campaign, or vote. Each party will have to:
- think of a name for itself
- decide on a candidate who will represent them
- organize a campaign to win votes
- decide on policies and what the party stands for (You need not restrict yourself to the policies of national political parties: you could choose policies of immediate interest to you and your friends. The main thing is to win votes.)
- publicize its point of view.

The candidate will probably be the main speech maker, but here are some things which party members could get involved in:
- interviewing voters and trying to find out where their vote will be cast
- designing posters, sandwich boards, leaflets, and badges
- organizing meetings at which the candidate will speak
- making sure that people who said they will support you actually turn out on polling day.

After everyone has voted, the Returning Officer counts the votes and announces the result.

### Was it fair?

In this country, elections are won on a 'first-past-the-post' basis. That is, whoever gets the most votes, wins. You may have a result in which **A** gets 12 votes, **B** gets 9 votes, and **C** gets 6 votes. **A** wins, even though 15 people (those who voted for **B** and **C**) voted against him or her.

Do you think this is fair?
If you think it's unfair, what other system could be used?

In your mock election, did anyone not bother to vote? Why was this?
What was the most important factor in winning votes? For example, was it the personality of the candidate? The effectiveness of the campaign? Or the policies of the party?

# 6 The law

## Contracts

A contract is an agreement between two or more people that something — for example a sale — shall take place. Some contracts are written down, but they don't have to be. You can agree to do something verbally, and it's still a contract. The most common contracts are for sales, hire purchase agreements, renting a house or flat, and employment.

### The advantages of a written contract

If what is agreed between you is written down, then you have a record to which you can both refer. If any argument arises about what was said, you can check.

### The disadvantages of a written contract

- You may feel obliged to sign something without having read it carefully first.
- The contract may be quite long and difficult to read.

### What to do if you are presented with a written contract

*Don't* sign it straight away. Ask if you can take it away to read. It's easier to read something when you're not being watched. If you don't understand what's in the contract, you can get help from the Citizens' Advice Bureau, or, if it's to do with a job, from the Careers Office or Jobcentre.

### Contract of employment

Every employee has a contract of employment with his or her employer. But it doesn't have to be written down. If you are offered a job by a firm verbally, told the rate of pay and what the job involves, and you accept the job, you have entered into a contract.

The law does not insist that the employment contract is in writing, but if you are a full-time worker, the employer *must* provide you with a written statement or written particulars within thirteen weeks of you starting work. You are a full-time employee if:

- you work sixteen hours a week or more
- you work between eight and sixteen hours a week, but have been in the same firm for five years.

**What's in the written statement:**
- The **names** of employer and employee.
- The **date** when employment began.
- The **rate of pay** or the method of calculating it, and whether it is to be paid by the week, month, or year.
- The **job title**. This need not be a full description of the job.
- **Holidays**. What are the holidays? Are they paid? When does the firm's holiday year begin?
- **Pension**. Is there a pension scheme? If so, what are the details?
- **Sick pay**. What are the firm's rules about sickness? You must make sure that you are clear what to do if you are sick. If you don't, you may lose sick pay. See page 81 for more details about statutory sick pay.
- **Notice**. The minimum periods of notice must be set out for both sacking and resignation.
- **Hours of work**. What is the normal working week? If there is compulsory overtime, the employer must say so.
- **Discipline at work**. You must be told what the disciplinary rules and procedures are. Sometimes you will be told that they are in a separate book, such as the works rules.
- **Complaints**. You should be told the name of the person you can go to if you've got a complaint.

Check the written statement carefully. If you sign it, you are bound to it; so if there's a mistake in it, you may lose out. If you need help, ask your union, the Department of Employment, the Citizens' Advice Bureau, the Careers Office, or a solicitor.

**The law says the employer must:**
- pay you.
- take reasonable care of you while you're at work, by providing a safe system of work.
- give you the benefits of your rights under the employment protection laws. So if you are eligible, you must be allowed to do things like claim maternity pay and get your job back after pregnancy; take time off for trade union duties or activities; be paid a guaranteed payment if you are laid off or put on short time.

**The law says you must:**
- turn up for work and work to a reasonable standard.
- obey orders. But you need only obey lawful orders; so if you are asked to do something like use an unsafe machine, or fiddle the books, you can and

should refuse. The orders must be within the terms of the employment contract. So if you are employed as a fitter, you need not obey an order to clean the toilets.

● take reasonable care when carrying out your duties.

## Rights at work

The longer you work for your employer, the more rights you have.

| Period of employment | Rights |
| --- | --- |
| 4 weeks | If you are sacked, you must be given at least one week's notice. |
| 13 weeks | You should be given written particulars of your contract of employment. |
| 26 weeks | If you are sacked, you can ask for a written statement of the reason for your sacking. |
| 1 year | You may be able to claim unfair dismissal if you are sacked. Seek advice first. |
| 2 years | If you are sacked you must be given two weeks' notice. You are entitled to redundancy pay. If you are being made redundant you can have reasonable time off to look for another job.<br>A woman is entitled to maternity pay and also to return to her job or an equivalent job after her baby is born. |
| 4–12 years | If you are sacked, you must be given one week's notice for each year of your employment. |
| over 12 years | If you are sacked, you must be given at least 12 weeks' notice. |

## Sales contracts

Any purchase or sale involves a contract. The contract does not have to be written down. Only contracts for the sale of land, hire purchase agreements, and some insurance agreements have to be written down.

A sales contract is being made here, because the customer has offered to buy the bread, and the shopkeeper has accepted the offer:

### When can I change my mind?
You can change your mind about buying something at any time before the money has been accepted by the person selling it; for example, before you've paid for something at the supermarket checkout.

If you're buying goods through mail order, the contract is made when the firm *posts* an acceptance, confirmation, goods, or receipt to the customer, *not* when the customer receives it. So you can usually only cancel goods ordered by post if you notify the company *before* they post the goods or a letter of acceptance.

When a shopkeeper makes a sale to a customer, he promises these things:
- the goods are fit for their usual use
- the goods are of proper quality
- the goods are as described
- what he says about the goods (his 'sales talk') is true.

So if you have any of the following complaints about the goods, the shopkeeper must do something about it:
'The goods don't work properly.'
'The goods don't work properly for the use I bought them for, which I told the shopkeeper about.'
'The goods work, but they are of poor quality.'
'There is nothing wrong with the goods, but they are not what I asked for.'
'The shopkeeper told me things about the goods which weren't true.'

The shopkeeper is not obliged to do anything about this complaint:
'There is nothing wrong with the goods, but I've changed my mind and I no longer want them.'

If you have bought goods which turn out to be faulty, the shop must replace them or refund your money. Go back to the shop and explain your complaint politely. If shop assistants are unhelpful, ask to speak to the manager. If he or she is unhelpful, you can get help and advice from the Citizens' Advice Bureau. In addition, some local authorities have set up Consumer Advice Centres. They will help with complaints, and may even support you if you have to take a shopkeeper to court. If you have a Consumer Advice Centre near you, ask them if they have someone who is prepared to come and talk to you about consumer rights.

The Consumers' Association is an independent body which advises and informs on consumer affairs. It publishes a magazine called *Which?* You can find copies of it in the library. *Which?* publishes information about different makes of goods, so that you can decide which is the best one for you.

### Buying from a private individual
A private individual who sells you something only promises that:
- the goods are as described
- what he says about the goods (his 'sales talk') is true.

# 📖 Discrimination

It is unlawful to discriminate against a person because of their
- race
- sex, or
- marital status.

'Discriminate' means to pick someone out and treat them differently. So **racial discrimination** is treating someone differently because they are, for example, black, or Asian, or Irish.

**Sexual discrimination** is treating someone differently because of their sex. It is more common for women to experience sexual discrimination than men.

**Marital discrimination** is treating someone differently because they are married. For example, a married woman might be discriminated against in a job application, because the employer is worried in case she leaves the job to have children.

Although discrimination is unlawful, it is not a **criminal** offence. The person discriminated against may be able to bring a **civil** claim for damages, but no criminal prosecution can be brought. This means that the police will not bring a case against someone who is guilty of discrimination. It is up to the individual to bring the case him- or herself.

The Race Relations Act of 1976 and the Sex Discrimination Act of 1975 provided two things:
1 They allow an individual to take legal action against someone who has discriminated against him or her.
2 They created watchdog bodies to monitor and advise on problems of discrimination. They are:

The Commission for Racial Equality
Elliott House
10–12 Allington Street
London SW1E 5EH

The Equal Opportunities Commission
Overseas House
Quay Street
Manchester M3 3HN

But the main responsibility for taking action against discrimination rests with the individual. Many people will simply not bother to take action. If they do, they must prove:
- that they have been discriminated against
- that it was unlawful discrimination within the terms of the Acts
- that the discrimination didn't come under one of the exceptions in the Acts. For example, a small firm with no more than five staff does not have to obey the sex and marital discrimination laws. Jobs in private houses, for example domestic jobs, are outside the Acts.

If you are thinking of taking action, it's best to get advice. The two Commissions mentioned above might help; or you could try the Citizens' Advice Bureau or, if you're in work, your Union.

1 What are some of the ways in which you might be discriminated against?
2 How would you know you were being discriminated against?
3 Do you think it would be easy to bring a claim of unlawful discrimination?
4 What would you do if you were discriminated against?

# The police

If you were mugged, or something belonging to you was stolen, you'd probably call the police, and expect them to help you. In order to fight crime, the police must be able to stop people, question them, and make enquiries.

### Helping the police

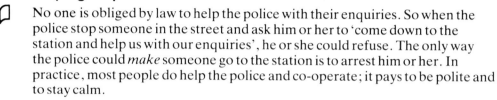

No one is obliged by law to help the police with their enquiries. So when the police stop someone in the street and ask him or her to 'come down to the station and help us with our enquiries', he or she could refuse. The only way the police could *make* someone go to the station is to arrest him or her. In practice, most people do help the police and co-operate; it pays to be polite and to stay calm.

The 1984 Police and Criminal Evidence Act came into force in 1986. It gives the police new powers in the areas of stop and search, arrest, and detention. The Act identifies the category of 'serious arrestable offence', such as rape, murder, kidnapping, and certain firearms and explosives offences. A 'serious arrestable offence' gives the police additional powers, such as delaying the suspect's right to have someone told of his arrest, or to consult a solicitor, for up to 36 hours. The Act also provides the citizen with extra safeguards against the misuse of their powers by the police.

### Statements

The police can question anyone, but their questions need not be answered. If there are grounds for suspecting that someone has committed an offence, the police should tell him or her that he or she need not say anything. If you are under 17, the police shouldn't ask you questions unless a parent or another adult is there.

### The right to see a solicitor

A suspect has the right to consult a solicitor, although in the case of a 'serious arrestable offence', the police superintendent can delay access to a solicitor for up to 36 hours.

### The right to have someone told of the arrest

A person under arrest who is being held at a police station is entitled to have someone told of his or her whereabouts as soon as practicable, unless it is a serious arrestable offence, when the police superintendent can authorize a delay of up to 36 hours.

## Fingerprints

You can refuse to have your fingerprints taken, but under some circumstances a police superintendent can authorize fingerprints to be taken without consent. Consent for children 10–14 is by their parents, and for young people 14–17, by themselves and their parents.

## Searching a person

A police officer can stop and search someone reasonably suspected of carrying illegal drugs, stolen goods, firearms, explosives, or 'prohibited articles'. A 'prohibited article' is an offensive weapon such as a bottle which has been purposely broken; an article made or adapted to use for theft, (e.g. a false-bottomed shopping bag), burglary, (e.g. a jemmy), or obtaining property by deception, (e.g. a false credit card). The Home Office draft code of conduct says that race, colour, or sex are not grounds for a search.

## What do you think?

Do you feel you know your local police? Read this article about a policeman who believes in community policing. Do you think his approach is a good one?

**TOP OF THE COPS**

'I just knock on the door and ask for a cup of tea'

**Award for Pc fighting crime with a cuppa**

BOBBY DAZZLER: Berinsfield youngsters get to grips with their friendly Pc Steven Hewson.

**THEY'VE** just pinned a medal on the jolly blue giant who fights crime with a cuppa.

For 6ft 6in Pc Steven Hewson has been given the chief constable's award for his work in Berinsfield, a notorious area for vandalism and crime.

Steve has won over villagers by his straight forward approach. "I've got to know everyone. I just

COPPER TEA: Steven with Mildred Godwin.

**By JEAN GORDON**

knock on their doors, say who I am and ask for a cup of tea.

"They're so taken aback that their reaction is to say: 'How many sugars do you take?'

"I sit myself down in their front room or kitchen and have a chat about anything.

"I can't say if crime has reduced in the two years I've been here, but the atmosphere is 100 per cent better.

"I run a police surgery once a week in the local school. It's known as the Blue Lamp Club."

And the door of his home at 2 Oxford Road, Dorchester, is constantly open to village youngsters.

"They come and pinch the apples from my tree in the Autumn." He is always popping in to the schools in the village.

"When he walks into school crowds of children rush up yelling "Watcha Steve."

"When I came here I visited the nursery school and the children wanted to draw round me so they could have a picture of their bobby.

"They had me lying on the floor and they were going round me with their crayons.

"Now they rush up to me in the street or playground and grab hold of my hand," said the 28 - year - old father of two.

"If ever I'm feeling down, I go into the playground and get cheered up.

"I believe in community policing. I come from Birmingham and I never saw a policeman on our estate unless there was trouble.

"In Berinsfield everyone knows I might be passing their front door.

"So they'd better not be up to anything.

"I know my approach is working when for example a girl came to me and told me she was addicted to glue sniffing and asked if I could help."

The Shrievalty Merit Award was presented by the High Sheriffs of Berkshire, Buckinghamshire and Oxfordshire this afternoon (Thursday).

## Talking to the police

It's more upsetting to be stopped and questioned by someone you don't know. People are likely to handle the situation badly, just because they are frightened. They might even behave in a guilty way — trying to run away, for example — even though they are perfectly innocent. How would you react if you were stopped and questioned by the police, and you hadn't done anything?

How do you think the police would respond to these reactions?
1 'You can't touch me, I know my rights.'
2 Running away.
3 'Why don't you do something useful, instead of pestering innocent people?'
4 'You're just picking on me.'
5 Silence.
6 'What would you like to know?'

Look at articles about the police and arrests in the newspapers. What can you say about the way the police are presented?

Ask if anyone in the group is prepared to talk about encounters they have had with the police.
● Why were they stopped?
● How did they think they handled the situation?
● If they think they handled it badly, what do they think they could have done to handle it better?

## Crime and young people

Criminal charges against children are heard in the Juvenile Court and not in the adult courts, such as the Magistrates' Court or Crown Court. The criminal responsibility of a child depends upon his or her age.

### Under 10
The child cannot be found guilty of a criminal offence, and so cannot be prosecuted. But the persistent offender may be put into the care of the local authority.

### 10 to 13
The child can only be found guilty of a criminal offence if it can be proved that he or she knew that what he or she was doing was wrong.

### 14 to 17
The child is subject to the same laws as an adult. It is assumed that he or she knows the law, and knows what is an offence. But he or she will usually be tried in the Juvenile Court, and if found guilty, is likely to receive a different sentence from the sentence an adult would be given.

### Over 17
The individual is an adult in the eyes of the law.

### Which court?

Most juveniles accused of crimes appear before the Juvenile Court. The bench will be made up of two or three magistrates drawn from a special panel of JPs (Justices of the Peace) who are supposed to have knowledge and experience of children. The procedure is similar to the Magistrates' Court. There is no jury. Only in cases of killing, or an offence where an adult might be given a sentence of fourteen years or more, might the magistrate decide that the child should be tried in a Crown Court with a jury.

If a juvenile is charged with a non-juvenile, both are likely to be tried together in an adult court.

If a child is 16 at the time of being charged, but 17 when the case comes to court, he is usually tried in the adult court.

### Attending a Juvenile Court hearing

The hearing is in private. The public cannot attend. A press reporter can be present, but the press cannot report the name, address, or school of the accused child, nor publish a photograph or any particulars which could identify anyone under 17.

### The causes and prevention of crime among young people

Most crimes committed by young people do not involve violence. Young offenders are most likely to have committed offences of theft, handling stolen goods, or burglary. Only 9% of juvenile offenders, and 15% of young adult offenders, have committed crimes involving violence, sex, or robbery. The peak age for convictions is 15 for boys and 14 for girls.

1 What do you think are the main reasons why young people commit crimes?
2 Could things be done to prevent young people committing crimes? For example:
   - should shop-lifting be made less easy through differently laid-out stores?
   - could housing estates be differently designed to prevent vandalism?
   - are there enough facilities for young people?

132

# Your rights and responsibilities

Take ten of the rights listed here. For each one, can you say what the responsibilities are that go with the right?

## How old do you have to be?

| | |
|---|---|
| **At birth** | • A bank or building society account can be opened in your name.<br>• You can own premium bonds. |
| **5** | • You must receive full-time education.<br>• You can drink alcohol in private. |
| **10** | • You can be convicted if it can be shown that you knew it was wrong. |
| **12** | • You can buy a pet. |
| **14** | • You can: take a part-time job.<br>      own an airgun.<br>      go into a bar with an adult, but cannot buy or consume<br>      alcoholic drink.<br>• If a boy, you can be convicted of rape or unlawful intercourse with a girl under 16. |
| **15** | • You can own a shotgun and ammunition. |
| **16** | • You can: marry with your parents' consent.<br>      apply for supplementary benefit.<br>      buy fireworks.<br>      choose your own doctor.<br>      join a trade union.<br>      drink beer, cider, porter or perry in a pub, but only with a meal in a part of a pub that serves meals, not at the bar.<br>      drive a moped or tractor.<br>      buy cigarettes.<br>• If a boy, you can join the armed forces if your parents agree.<br>• If a girl, you can consent to sexual intercourse. |
| **17** | • You can: drive a car or motorcycle.<br>      go into a betting shop, but not bet.<br>      have an airgun in a public place.<br>• If a girl, you can join the armed forces if your parents agree. |
| **18** | • You become an adult and can:<br>      vote.<br>      marry without parental consent.<br>      change your name.<br>      apply for a passport.<br>      obtain credit.<br>      be eligible for jury service.<br>      buy drinks in the bar of a pub.<br>      be tattooed.<br>      donate blood and organs.<br>      bet.<br>      join the armed forces without parental consent. |
| **21** | • You can: stand in a general or local election.<br>      apply for a liquor licence.<br>      if male, consent to homosexual acts in private.<br>      drive a lorry or bus. |

# 7 Health

## What is health?

**?** Do you think health is something over which you have any control? To find out, see if you agree or disagree with the following statements:

1 Being healthy is just a question of not being ill.
2 It's bad luck if you fall ill. There's nothing you can do to prevent it.
3 A person's state of health is connected with the way he or she lives; for example, how much exercise they take, what their diet is like, whether they smoke, drink, or take drugs.
4 The jobs which some people do might damage their health if they didn't take wise precautions and follow the safety regulations.
5 Some people live more dangerously and take more risks than others.
6 Your health can be affected by things like bad housing, worries, and stress.

Now give your definition of a healthy person and an unhealthy person by finishing these sentences:

1 A healthy person is someone who . . .
2 The healthiest person I know is . . . because he/she . . .
3 The unhealthiest person I know is . . . because he/she . . .

**?** What risks to their health are these people taking?

134

Most people are interested in their health. There's usually something every day on television or in the newspapers about some aspect of health. Collect any articles or information about programmes which you see. How many of the articles are to do with each of the following?

1  Health and beauty — diets, skin care, hair care.
2  Not getting ill; for example, preventing heart disease and cancer, watching your weight, and taking exercise.
3  Coping with and caring for sick relatives at home; for example, the elderly or young children.
4  Industrial accidents.
5  Chemicals which cause disease.
6  Accidents in the home, such as fire, gas and electricity faults, or accidental poisoning.
7  Environmental health hazards, such as the problems of nuclear waste, pollution, or poor housing.
8  The tragic effects of drug overdoses, alcoholism, or solvent abuse.
9  The possible dangerous side effects of some drugs which are prescribed by the doctor.
10  Cuts in health service provision.
11  Expensive and difficult surgical operations, such as transplants.

### Advertisements

Many advertisements appeal to our interest in staying healthy. They can do this either quite openly, or in a sly way. They often appeal to the emotions.
 Look for advertisements which:
- say openly that the product is good for you
- imply that the product is good for you by using words such as 'natural', 'healthy', 'full of goodness', 'full of fitness'
- appeal to the emotions as, for example, advertisements for low-cholestrol margarine often do
- appeal to people's vanity or their wish to look different from the way they do now.

# Nutrition and healthy living

For most of us, eating is a source of pleasure. We use food to celebrate special occasions, as a reward, or as comfort. It's often easy to forget the importance of eating properly, and that what we eat or don't eat affects our health.

Think of as many festive occasions through the year as you can. What food is associated with each one?

Can you remember occasions when you, or someone you know, were offered something to eat as a reward, or as comfort? What were the occasions?

## The health connection

Eating too many of the wrong sorts of food can lead to health problems. Being overweight, being anaemic, having tooth decay, and constipation, are some of the results of poor diet. Heart disease and high blood pressure are also linked to diet.

## Changes we ought to make in our diet

Medical experts now think we should:

- eat less sugar. This means less sugar in drinks and on food. It also means less cakes, biscuits, puddings, sweets, and fizzy drinks.
- eat less fat, particularly animal fat. Some foods are obviously fatty, such as butter, margarine, lard, suet, cooking oils, fat on meat, and fried foods. But there is also a considerable amount of fat in foods like pastry, cakes, biscuits, chocolate, salad cream, nuts, milk, cream, cheese, pork, bacon, ham, and sausages.
- eat more foods which are rich in fibre. This means eating wholemeal flour and bread rather than white flour and bread; eating bran or wholewheat cereal; eating plenty of peas, beans, lentils, and root vegetables, as well as dried and fresh fruit.

➡ Think of ten foods which contain a lot of sugar, ten foods which are fatty, and ten foods which are high in fibre.
Write down what you ate at each meal yesterday. How many of the foods were high in fat or sugar? How many were high in fibre? Look back at the list you made of foods connected with special occasions. How many of them are high in fat or sugar?

❓ What would you say is wrong with this packed lunch:
> two rounds of chocolate spread sandwich made with white bread
> one packet of crisps
> four chocolate biscuits?

What changes could be made to the packed lunch to make it more healthy?

Which of these foods fit in with the guidelines for healthy eating?
Which would you choose to eat yourself?
> fried fish and chips
> cheese salad and a wholemeal roll
> chocolate sponge and custard
> beefburger in a white roll
> low-fat yogurt
> grilled fish, boiled potatoes, grilled tomatoes
> fried sausages, eggs, fried white bread
> chicken, baked potatoes, peas
> muesli

Think of as many advertisements as you can for food, sweets, and drinks. How many of the foods and drinks fit into the guidelines for healthy eating?

## Looking after teeth

Eating too much sugar and sweet things can cause tooth decay. What could you eat instead of sweet things that would be less harmful to your teeth? Looking after your teeth also means cleaning them at least twice a day and visiting the dentist for a check-up every six months. Do you?

## Exercise

List all the ways in which you take exercise now. How many of the things like games, sports, dance, or gymnastics take place in school?
   Medical experts believe we should take more exercise. But when people leave school they usually take much less exercise, or stop altogether. Why do you think this is?

Ask people you know who left school recently if they still play a sport. If they don't, ask them why they've stopped.

## Sleep

❓ A recent survey shows that many young people feel they don't get enough sleep. Do you feel short of sleep (**a**) often (**b**) sometimes (**c**) hardly ever? If you don't get enough sleep, why is this? On days after going without enough sleep, how do you feel? How is your ability to work affected? Do you find it difficult to concentrate in lessons?

## Using your doctor

Do you know how to contact your doctor? Do you feel happy about consulting him or her? Can you tell when a situation is an emergency and needs immediate treatment? To find out, answer these questions:

1 What is the name of your doctor?
2 Is he or she part of a large practice or a small practice?
3 Where is the surgery?
4 What are the surgery hours?
5 What is the telephone number of the surgery?
6 How do you contact your doctor outside surgery hours — say in the middle of the night?
7 Do you usually go to see your doctor on your own, or does a parent or other adult go with you?
8 If an adult goes with you, does he or she tell the doctor what's wrong, or do you?

A lot of minor illnesses can be treated successfully at home, or don't need any treatment at all. So how do you know when you're ill enough to need a doctor?

In which of these cases would you think you should see a doctor? You have:
1 a headache
2 a cold and sore throat
3 a cold, sore throat, temperature, and aching limbs
4 a stomach upset that has lasted for more than 36 hours
5 a sudden unexplainable attack of stomach ache
6 a fainting fit
7 blurred vision
8 a dog bite which has broken the skin and caused bleeding

Would you call the doctor in the circumstances listed below? Some of them might be real emergencies; in which would it be best to dial 999 and ask for an ambulance?
1 Your baby sister comes in carrying a bottle which she has found underneath the sink. It looks as though she's been drinking from it, but you can't tell what's in the bottle.
2 While you're baby-sitting for friends, their child is sick.
3 Your mother passes out in the kitchen and you can't bring her round.
4 Your dad cuts himself in the workshop.
5 A man is knocked off his bicycle and is lying unconscious in the road.

## Explaining things to the doctor

Not many people like having to tell the doctor what's wrong with them. Sometimes it can be embarrassing; sometimes you're afraid of sounding foolish. Or you might be worried that something serious is wrong.

**?** Have there been times when you've had difficulty in telling the doctor what was wrong with you?

What situations can you imagine when other people might find it difficult to talk to their doctor?

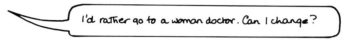

My doctor's quite old. When I go to him, I can never explain myself properly, and I feel a fool. He sits there behind a big desk and doesn't say anything. I always have to start talking first.

An important part of what doctors do is to listen to their patients. The doctor is probably waiting for you to talk to him or her, and is sympathetic. Before you go to your doctor, perhaps you could practise saying what's wrong with you; either on your own, or to a friend.

I'd rather go to a woman doctor. Can I change?

Over the age of 16, you can change your GP for any reason, and you do not have to explain the reason. But under the age of 16, the choice of a doctor is made for you by your mother, father, or guardian.

The Family Practitioner Committee, The Community Health Council, and the Citizens' Advice Bureau all have a list of National Health Service General Practitioners. Choose which doctor or practice you want to register with; perhaps ask friends and neighbours whom they recommend. Telephone the practice and ask the receptionist if you can be accepted as a patient. Occasionally, some doctors' lists are full.

Do I have any say in whether I'm examined or treated?

You cannot be examined or treated without your consent. The only exceptions to this are if you have a notifiable infectious disease, which others might catch, or if you have been detained under the Mental Health Act.

If your doctor asks you to give your consent to treatment, he or she must tell you of any risks involved.

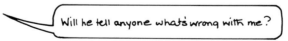

Will he tell anyone what's wrong with me?

Usually, doctors can pass on information about you only when you've given your permission, unless it is to other professionals involved in treating you.

Children have the same right as adults to consult any doctor confidentially. But in the case of children under 16 wanting to consult a doctor without their parents being told, the doctor is in a difficult position. The doctor has to weigh up his or her responsibility to both the child and the parents or guardians.

If the doctor cannot persuade the child that parents or guardians should be involved, he or she may decide to give treatment without parental consent.

# Contraception

### Doctors and contraception

It is now legal for a girl under sixteen to go for contraceptive advice and information to her doctor, or to any suitable clinic. For a time, Mrs Victoria Gillick's campaign meant that doctors who gave contraceptive advice to under-sixteens without their parents' consent were breaking the law. Young people were clearly put off from going to their doctor or clinic. The Family Planning Association says that they have no doubt that this has resulted in an increase in the number of teenage pregnancies, and in pregnancies among the under-sixteens.

Now the law has been changed. It is not illegal for a girl under sixteen to go, without her parent's consent, to a doctor or clinic for advice on contraception. The doctor will probably try to persuade the girl to involve her parents, but this is no longer a legal requirement.

The message is clear: Don't be afraid to go for help. If you think you need advice or information, go now.

If you don't want to go to your doctor for advice on contraception, you can go to a Family Planning Clinic, or a young people's clinic run by the Brook Advisory Service. Look for the name of your local clinic under 'Family Planning' in your telephone directory or Yellow Pages. You can also get free leaflets and information from:

The Family Planning Information Service
27–35 Mortimer St
London W1N 7RJ
*Telephone*: 01–636 7866.

A clinic is a good place to go to for help and advice on contraception. If you are prescribed the contraceptive pill, the clinic will tell your family doctor for health reasons.

They'll talk to you about things that you're worried about, not just contraception.

One reason why I prefer to go to the clinic is that it provides a specialist service, and I don't feel I'm wasting the doctor's time when I'm not ill.

They encouraged my boyfriend to come too.

Contraceptives from clinics and your family doctor are free, although men are unlikely to get sheaths free.

Here is a list of which contraceptives are available from where:

|  | Clinic | Doctor | Chemist |
|---|---|---|---|
| pill | yes | yes | not without prescription |
| sheath | yes | no | yes |
| cap | yes | yes | no |
| IUD | yes | yes | no |
| spermicide | yes | yes | yes |

Do you know what these methods are and how they work?

### The contraceptive pill

The pill is taken by the girl. It works by altering her hormone balance so that she doesn't ovulate (that is, she doesn't produce an egg). Most girls are prescribed a pill which is taken every day for three weeks, followed by a week's break. During the week when she is not taking the pill, she will have a period, which may well be lighter than she is used to.

**Are there any side effects?**

There may be. The doctor or clinic will see the girl regularly and check things like weight and blood pressure.

**How effective is it?**

If it's taken regularly, the pill is the most reliable form of contraception. But if the girl forgets to take her pill, the level of protection goes down, and she must use other methods for the rest of the month.

### The coil or IUD (intra-uterine device)

This is a small piece of plastic or metal with a thread attached to it. It is inserted into the womb and stays there until taken out by the doctor. Its presence in the womb stops the egg from settling and growing into a baby.

This is often not the best method of contraception for young girls. More often, it's fitted in women who have already had a child.

**Are there any side effects?**

It sometimes leads to heavier or longer periods.

**How effective is it?**

Only 2% of women who used this method for a year would get pregnant.

### The cap

This is a rubber dome. A ring of wire inside the rubber keeps it in a circular shape.

The girl puts the cap into her vagina, so that it covers the entrance to the womb. It prevents sperm from entering the womb. To make it extra effective, she puts spermicide (a cream which kills sperm) on the cap before inserting it. The nurse or doctor at the clinic will show you how to put the cap in. If it's properly in place, you can't feel it's there. There are no side effects from this method.

**How effective is it?**

Only 3% of women who used this method properly for a year would get pregnant.

### Sheath, condom, or French letter

This is a close-fitting rubber contraceptive which the boy puts on to his erect penis before intercourse. If he also uses a spermicide cream, or the girl puts spermicide into her vagina, the sheath is a more effective contraceptive. The sperm are caught in the sheath, and the boy must take care not to spill any when he removes the sheath. There are no side effects. Using a sheath gives some protection against catching a sexually transmitted disease.

**How effective is it?**

Only 3% of women whose partner used this method properly for a year would get pregnant.

### The rhythm method

The girl calculates the time in her monthly cycle when she is ovulating (releasing an egg which could be fertilized by sperm and grow into a baby). The clinic or her doctor can teach her how to calculate this. She and her partner do not have sex during this time. It is the only method of contraception permitted by the Roman Catholic Church.

**How effective is it?**

It is extremely unreliable for young people, since a girl's periods are often irregular.

## The vaginal contraceptive sponge

This is on sale from chemists. It is a sponge impregnated with spermicide which the woman inserts in her vagina. It is not recommended for a girl who wishes to be sure of not getting pregnant, since the failure rate is high.

## Withdrawal

This depends on the boy withdrawing his penis from the girl's vagina before he ejaculates and releases sperm.

**How effective is it?**

It is very unreliable, since some sperm may leak from the boy's penis even before ejaculation.

## The 'morning-after' pill

This is prescribed by some doctors and clinics for girls who have had unprotected sex within the previous 48 hours. It is *not* for regular contraceptive use.

## Sterilization

Some people who have had their families choose to be sterilized. Sterilization is not suitable for young people, since it is difficult to reverse, and would probably mean that they couldn't have children.

**?** Now you've read the information above, answer these questions:
1 Which methods of birth control can only be got from a doctor or clinic?
2 Which can be got from a chemist?
3 Which methods are the girl's responsibility?
4 Which are the boy's?
5 How many methods depend on the co-operation of both partners?
6 Which methods are suitable for the following people? Which methods would *not* be suitable for them?
   a A couple with one child who want to wait before conceiving again.
   b A strict Roman Catholic couple.
   c A girl and her partner who have a steady sexual relationship.
   d A girl who has occasional sex.
   e A boy who has occasional sex.
7 Put the methods of birth control described above into their order of effectiveness.

Many old wives' tales abound, such as the belief that you can't get pregnant if you do it standing up, you can't get pregnant if it's the first time, and so on.
**?** They are untrue. Have you heard any such stories? What are they?

# Sexually transmitted diseases (STDs)

 These are diseases which are spread by sexual contact and intimacy. If neither partner has sex with anyone else, and if neither partner has an STD, neither can catch it from the other. STDs cannot be caught from lavatory seats or bedding or clothes.

## Symptoms and effects of STDs

| Disease | Symptoms in men | Symptoms in women | Long-term consequences |
|---|---|---|---|
| Gonorrhoea | A burning pain when passing water; smelly discharge from penis. | May detect a heavy vaginal discharge and some pain: 70% have no symptoms. | Sterility: that is, the inability to conceive or father children. |
| Non-specific urethritis (NSU) | Same as gonorrhoea. | Does not occur in women. | If untreated, can lead to painful complications. |
| Pelvic inflammatory disease (PID) | Does not occur in men. | Acute or burning pain. | Can lead to sterility if untreated. |
| Herpes | Sores like cold sores on the sex organs | | May vanish but reappear |
| Syphilis | Painless sores on or inside the sex organs | | If untreated, can lead to insanity, blindness, paralysis, and death. |
| Trichimonas vaginalis | Does not occur in men. | Yellow, smelly vaginal discharge, pain, itchiness and sore sex organs. | |
| Warts | Appear on the sex organs | | Do not disappear like ordinary warts. If untreated, will spread and may lead to other infections. |
| Scabies | Tiny parasites which burrow under the skin and lay eggs. | | May cause secondary infections. |
| Lice | Tiny parasites which stick on the pubic hair and cause itching. | | |
| Candidiosis (thrush) | A red penis which is sore at the tip. Not always caught sexually. It can be caused by certain medicines. | Thick vaginal discharge, a sore and itchy vagina. Not always caught sexually. It can be caused by certain medicines. | |

## Facts about STDs

1 People who start their sex life early and who have many changes of partners are at much greater risk of catching an STD.
2 Most STDs can be cured if they are treated as soon as the symptoms are noticed. The longer you wait, the more difficult the treatment.
3 A person can be a carrier without having any symptoms.
4 If you or your partner think something is wrong, you should stop having sex. Both of you should go to the special clinic for a check-up.
5 Pain on passing water, or an unpleasant discharge, do not necessarily mean you have an STD. But you should go to a doctor anyway, since something is wrong which should be put right.

**6** Special clinics deal with STDs. You can go to them if you don't want to go to your doctor. Telephone your local hospital to find the address and time of your nearest clinic. You do not need an appointment, and nobody is told that you have been unless you give your permission.

**?** How can you avoid catching an STD?
What should you do if you think there is something wrong?

# Smoking

### Facts about smoking

Smoking damages your health. Of people aged 35 and over, more than twice as many smokers as non-smokers die before reaching the age of 65.

Smoking is responsible for a lot of ill-health and absenteeism at work. About 50 million working days a year are lost in Britain through diseases which are connected with smoking.

**?** Can you name some diseases connected with smoking? Most people know about heart disease and lung cancer, but did you know that smoking also increases the risk of:
- strokes
- bronchitis
- cancer of the mouth or throat
- cancer of the bladder
- stomach ulcers
- serious gum infections and tooth loss
- diseases of the arteries of the legs?

The risk of death from lung cancer is related to the number of cigarettes smoked and the age of starting smoking.

Under the age of 65, smokers are about twice as likely to die of coronary heart disease as non-smokers; heavy smokers are about three times as likely to die of coronary heart disease.

Most people who smoke start in childhood or adolescence. If you are a non-smoker until you are 20, you're unlikely to start.

Children who smoke are more likely to have colds. They get out of breath more easily, and are twice as likely to be off sick from school.

Pregnant women who smoke are more likely to have a miscarriage, and more likely to have an underweight baby.

If you are a non-smoker, but in a room with heavy smokers, you will inhale the equivalent of several cigarettes in an hour.

In 1979 the National Health Service spent £155 million treating patients with smoking-related diseases.

About £100 million a year is spent on advertising cigarettes and tobacco.

Tobacco is one of the most harmful of the addictive drugs. The things which do most harm are:
- **tar**, which damages the breathing tubes and lungs.
- **carbon monoxide**, a gas which cuts down the amount of oxygen carried in the blood. It also damages the heart and arteries.
- **nicotine**, which is an addictive drug. It causes over-activity of the heart and narrows the arteries.

## So why do people smoke?

Make a list of the reasons these people have given for smoking. Can you think of other reasons people might give? Do they seem to you good reasons? Think of an argument *against* each reason.

Interview someone you know who smokes. Ask them:
- why they started smoking
- when they had their first cigarette
- what it felt like to smoke for the first time
- whether they've ever tried to give up
- what happened when they tried to give up
- whether they wish they could give up now
- whether they would encourage or discourage a young person from starting to smoke
- what effect they think smoking has on their health
- whether they get breathless after exercise or running upstairs
- whether they wake up with a cough in the mornings
- whether they seem to take longer to get over coughs and colds than non-smokers do
- how much they spend on cigarettes
- what other people — for example their family or friends or colleagues at work — think about their smoking. Do people avoid them when they light up?
- whether they know how harmful cigarettes are. What good things do they think they get from smoking, if any?

---

**The good news**
- In a recent survey of people who had given up smoking, two out of three said they found it surprisingly easy.
- Smoking is declining in this country.
- If you do give up smoking, you may reverse the damage you do yourself.

---

## How non-smokers feel about smoking

▶ Make a list of the reasons these people have given for not smoking, and for their dislike of others smoking. Were you surprised at any of the things they said?

 Role-play the following situations from these people's stories:
Where the young couple are trying to prevent the grandmother smoking over the baby.
How do you think the young couple feel?
How do you think the grandmother feels?
Has the baby got any rights?

Where the boy and his girlfriend are breaking up because of her smoking.
How do you think the girlfriend feels? Will she stop smoking now?

# Drinking

Why do people drink alcohol?
Is it difficult to refuse?
If so, why?

📖 **Facts about drinking**

- Spirits (brandy, whisky, gin, vodka, or rum) contain about 40% alcohol.
- Fortified wine (sherry, port, or vermouth) contains about 20% alcohol.
- Table wine (75 centilitres) contains about 10% alcohol.
- Beer contains about 5% alcohol.

These amounts of drink are about the same in the quantity of alcohol they contain:

Half a pint of beer equals one glass of table wine, equals one glass of sherry, equals 1 single measure of spirits. All these drinks contain the equivalent of one unit of alcohol.

An adult man's body can cope with a maximum of six units a day. An adult woman's body can cope with a maximum of four units a day, since on average, women weigh 20% less than men. Many doctors advise that a pregnant woman should give up drinking altogether, since otherwise she may risk damaging her unborn child. Young drinkers should not go above half the adult amounts. Remember, these are *upper limits*, not recommended amounts.

The amount of alcohol that a person can safely drink will depend on other things, such as:
- how quickly a person drinks
- when he or she last ate
- how accustomed he or she is to alcohol
- whether he or she is taking other drugs.

## How does alcohol affect the way people behave?

This table shows the effects of blood alcohol levels on an average man. Young people are likely to experience these effects after *much less* than the table shows.

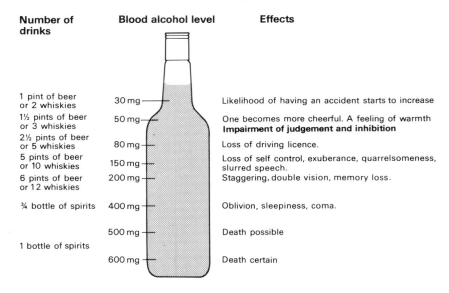

| Number of drinks | Blood alcohol level | Effects |
|---|---|---|
| 1 pint of beer or 2 whiskies | 30 mg | Likelihood of having an accident starts to increase |
| 1½ pints of beer or 3 whiskies | 50 mg | One becomes more cheerful. A feeling of warmth **Impairment of judgement and inhibition** |
| 2½ pints of beer or 5 whiskies | 80 mg | Loss of driving licence. |
| 5 pints of beer or 10 whiskies | 150 mg | Loss of self control, exuberance, quarrelsomeness, slurred speech. |
| 6 pints of beer or 12 whiskies | 200 mg | Staggering, double vision, memory loss. |
| ¾ bottle of spirits | 400 mg | Oblivion, sleepiness, coma. |
| | 500 mg | Death possible |
| 1 bottle of spirits | | |
| | 600 mg | Death certain |

Young people are more easily affected by alcohol than older people.

Write or draw a story, or write a play, about what happens to this group of people when they go out to the pub one night:

Sonia, a fifteen-year-old who knows she is under age to drink in a pub, but thinks that it is cool to order spirits. She can't tolerate much alcohol.

Des is her older brother. He refuses to be persuaded into drinking more than he wants to. He doesn't think Sonia should drink spirits, but thinks perhaps it's time she learnt a lesson.

Andy is a fried of Des. He regards himself as able to hold his alcohol. He offers to buy Sonia spirits, and thinks he's safe on a motorbike even after drinking.

### How would you cope?

What would you do in the following situations?
1 People are pressing you to drink, even though you're under age and you really don't want one.
2 At a party you go to, there don't seem to be any soft drinks offered. You don't want to drink any alcohol.
3 One of your friends has drunk too much and is becoming embarrassing. He or she wants to go on drinking; you think it's time to go home.
4 Someone who has clearly had too much to drink is offering you a lift home.

## The law says that if you are:

- under 5, you are not allowed to drink alcohol, even at home, unless prescribed by a doctor
- under 14, you are not allowed in bars, but you are allowed in rooms in pubs where drink is not sold, and in restaurants where drink is served with food
- 14 or 15, you are allowed in bars, but cannot drink alcohol
- 16 or 17, you are allowed to drink beer, cider, or perry in a part of a pub where drink is not sold
- 18 and over, you can buy and drink alcohol.

It is illegal for anyone to buy alcohol in a pub bar for someone under 18, and it is illegal to sell alcohol to anyone under 18 in a pub, off licence, or supermarket.

Some people argue that the rigid licensing laws in this country, and the laws governing the age at which drinking is allowed, actually encourage people to drink more than they would otherwise do. What do you think?

Here is a common situation arising between a teenager and his concerned parents:

John's parents are worried about the group of friends he goes around with. They are older than he is, and drink quite heavily. John himself is under age. The parents consider the following actions:

- to forbid John to go out with his friends
- to allow him to go out, but to forbid him to drink alcoholic drinks
- to demand to know where he's going, so that they can drop in at the pub later
- to invite the friends in for a drink and a chat
- to talk to John about the dangers of drinking under age and when he's not used to it.

Say what you think John's reaction would be to each of the above courses of action. Which do think would be the most helpful thing the parents could do?

# Drugs and drug abuse

Many of the drugs we take are potentially harmful and addictive, but they are legal and socially acceptable. It would be hard to find someone who had never taken coffee, tea, aspirin, coca cola (which contains caffeine), tobacco, alcohol, or some prescribed drug such as sleeping pills or tranquillizers.
List some of the reasons why people take any of the above drugs. Could some of the same reasons explain why some young people take illegal drugs?

In a recent publication, the Health Education Council lists sixteen reasons why young people take drugs. They are:

1  Drugs are available.
2  To please a friend.
3  They feel empty inside.
4  They've no one to rely on.
5  Because they want to be accepted by a peer group that uses drugs.
6  They feel angry or violent.
7  Because they have very poor relationships with their parents.
8  For fun.
9  Because they feel miserable and confused.
10  Because they are confused sexually.
11  Out of curiosity.
12  Because they feel cut off from family and friends.
13  Because they can't tolerate frustration.
14  To rebel against parents.
15  Because they feel worthless and out of place.
16  Because they cannot relate to other people.

**?** The most common reasons why teenagers take drugs are to do with experimenting and finding out. Which six of the reasons listed above are to do with experimenting and finding out?
Which reasons suggest that the teenager is trying drugs to escape depression?

## Mary's story

Mary has made a big effort, and with the help of drugs counsellors, has managed to come off drugs. She says:

I was taking acid twice a week and it was making me go crazy. I knew what it was like to go mad. If you take LSD too regularly you end up on heroin. Then you're dead.

When I used to take drugs a lot, I didn't have enough money, so I did some shoplifting and got caught. That's when I began to realize I needed help to give up. I know worse things that have happened to people who are desperate for money to buy drugs. Teenage prostitution, for example. Now I'm just really grateful that I managed to stop in time.

What risks to her health was Mary aware of?
Apart from health risks, what other risks does she mention?
Mary says that if you get on to heroin, 'You're dead.' Look at the table
below. What are the effects of heroin? Mary thinks her fifteen-year-old sister
is experimenting with drugs. What would she say to her sister?

## Drugs: how they affect you

| Drug type | Short-term effects | Some hazards and long-term effects |
| --- | --- | --- |
| 1 Morphine, Opium, Heroin | Can relieve pain and anxiety. Can cause great excitement. | Dependence and addiction. Dangerous if taken with other drugs. Deaths are caused by infections from dirty needles; choking on vomit; suicide or overdose. |
| 2 Sedatives, Barbiturates, Downers | Calm anxiety. High doses have similar effects to alcohol. | Alcohol and barbiturates taken together kill. Suicide and overdosing may occur. |
| 3 Amphetamines, Uppers, Speed | Can produce excitement and happiness. | Injecting massive doses can cause terrifying feelings and brief psychosis. |
| 4 Cocaine | Similar to amphetamines. | Toxic if taken in high doses. |
| 5 Cannabis, Marijuana, Hashish, Ganja | Reddened eyes, dilated pupils, unsteady walk, a dry mouth. There may be a feeling of restlessness followed by a feeling of great happiness. Things may seem to alter in appearance. Time may seem to speed up or stand still. These sensations may be very alarming to some people. | It is not addictive, but may lead to experimenting with more dangerous drugs. |
| 6 Hallucinogens: Mescalin, LSD | Affects the way people see things. | May be a terrifying experience. Suicide. Overdose can lead to death. |

Is drug abuse a problem in your area? What agencies exist to help drug
addicts in your area? Contact them and ask if a drugs counsellor would be
willing to come and talk to you about his or her work.

### Glue-sniffing (solvent abuse)

Glue-sniffing is a relatively recent form of drug abuse in this country. It is
estimated that up to 10% of pupils aged between 12 and 16 are involved in
solvent abuse in some British schools. About 45 to 50 young people, mostly
teenage boys, die each year as a result of sniffing glue or other solvents.

The **short-term effects** are similar to those of alcohol. Sniffing glue may
produce drowsiness, hallucinations, and loss of consciousness. The **long-
term effects** are not fully known, but solvent-sniffers frequently become
listless and apathetic. They develop a rash on their faces, and cold
symptoms. Accidents occur because of choking and suffocation, through the
use of plastic bags and/or inhaling vomit. This is how the deaths occur,
together with such accidents as falling off high buildings.

**?** Do you think the reasons for sniffing glue are the same as those listed above for taking other drugs?

There are some major differences between solvent sniffing and taking other drugs:
1 It is not illegal.
2 The things you need to be able to do it are easily available.
3 It is much less expensive.

**?** So what can be done to discourage solvent abuse? In Scotland, two shopkeepers have been convicted for selling glue-sniffing kits to children. They were jailed for three years under a Scottish common law provision which has no equivalent in England. At the moment, the government is not considering making glue-sniffing a criminal offence.

**?** Why do you think the government is not making glue-sniffing illegal? What would be the difficulties of making it illegal to sell glue-sniffing kits (usually a polythene bag with glue)?

If you were a shopkeeper and some young people came into your shop to buy glue and aerosol cans and polythene bags, what would you do? What would you say to a friend who was talking about trying it? What would you say to someone who tried to persuade you to try it?

SOLVENT ABUSE

We reserve the right *not* to supply certain solvent-based products.

STOP SOLVENT ABUSE KILLS

# 8 Deciding

This chapter is about things which most people find very difficult:
- thinking about and solving problems
- deciding things for yourself
- making your own judgements.

You may already have found that you seem to have more problems to solve than when you were younger. If you haven't had to already, you will soon be asked to make decisions which may affect your future and the rest of your life; how do you know what the right decisions are? You may already find yourself questioning other people's judgements, and wanting to disagree with what they say. And this may lead to conflicts and fights with people with whom you used to get on well — perhaps your parents or your teachers. At the same time, your friends and other people in your age group will be exploring different experiences. They may press you to join in. You have to decide whether you're going to, and what the risks are if you do or don't join in.

Of course, the three areas — problems, decisions, and judgements — are not clear cut and separate; they overlap. So solving problems usually involves taking decisions and making judgements. But we're going to look at the areas separately, to see if we can understand them better.

# Solving problems

Some problems are fairly easy to deal with; these are the ones which are caused by not knowing how to do something, or where to get help, or even that help is available.

## Solving problems caused by lack of information

The good thing about these sorts of problems is that they can usually be solved if you:
- know where to go for help
- know how to ask for help
- don't mind being persistent until you get what you want.

Of course, you can still worry a lot about problems like these; but if you solve them, you feel good! Can you sort out which of the problems in this list could be solved if you knew where to go for help?

1 You'd like a book on bike maintenance, but you can't afford to buy one.
2 You'd like to learn how to look after your bike.
3 You can't decide whether to walk or take a bus.
4 You don't know what to buy your sister for her birthday.
5 You and your dad don't get on as well as you used to.
6 You can't do your school homework.
7 You want to find out about youth hostelling in Wales.
8 You need more money.
9 You want to know where your nearest youth club is.
10 You want to learn Kung Fu.
11 You're worried about your health.

What do you think are the most common problems which affect your age group? Write them down. Compare your list with a neighbour's.
Are any of them the same?
Can they be divided into groups?
Are some of them to do with the same sorts of things?
How many do you think can be solved easily?
How many do you know how to solve?
Are any of your practical problems — e.g. difficulties with travel, poor employment prospects — to do with the area in which you live?

## Knowing where to get help

There are many agencies whose job it is to provide advice and information. Sometimes it's obvious from their names what problems they can help with. But often they can help with a wide range of queries, some of which may surprise you. Try to visit these places:

| | |
|---|---|
| the library | a post office |
| the Citizens' Advice Bureau | a bank |
| the Careers Office | the College of Further Education. |

Collect any free leaflets they have, particularly those relating to students and school leavers. If someone is prepared to talk to you, ask them what sort of problems they help people with. Then answer these questions:

What can the DHSS help with?

Where would you go for advice about returning some faulty goods?

Who could help you with a housing problem?

What work-related courses for school leavers does your local college run?

What services does the bank offer school leavers and students?

## Knowing how to ask

Knowing where to go for help is only one part of the solution; you still have to ask for what you want. So now, with a partner, practise asking for the help or information that you need in each of these situations:

1 You want to find out about evening classes on cooking in a bedsit.
2 You think your landlord is charging you too much rent.
3 You want to open a bank account.

At the end, your partner should tell you if you were:
- reasonably polite in your manner
- able to say what you wanted clearly.

Sometimes you go to the right place and ask the right question, and still don't get the help you're looking for!

What should the person do in each of the situations below?

## Practical problems

People have different practical problems at different stages of their lives.

Think back to when you were younger. What problems can you remember having then? Do you still have these problems? If they have been resolved, do they seem very serious when you look back on them?
If you have a younger brother or sister, what problems do they seem to have? What is your view of their problems?
Have you ever thought about problems your parents might have? What do they seem to be?

Here are some stories about people older than you are. What would you say their problems are?

1 Jill and Andy got married because Jill was pregnant. They were very happy to start with. They have a bedsit in Jill's mother's house. They thought perhaps Jill's parents would help with the baby when it was born. After the baby arrived, Jill's mother became more interfering. She upsets Jill by telling her what to do all the time. Jill's father has started asking when they're going to get a place on their own. Jill feels tired all the time. Andy's constantly worried about money. He wonders why he and Jill never go out any more. And he's heard there are to be redundancies at his firm.

2 Mrs Davies' children have now all left home. Before, she never seemed to have enough time to herself. Now the day drags. Her home is easy to keep tidy. Her husband is quite happy in his job and hobbies, and doesn't seem to have noticed anything wrong. Mrs Davies has started feeling depressed and lonely. She notices that a glass or two of sherry at lunch time helps to pass the day.

3 Paul has been in the same job for seven years. Everyone at work is very pleasant, and he quite likes the job. But he knows that he can't get any further without management training. Sometimes he mentions it to his employer, but he keeps being passed over.

## Solving problems which worry you

Worrying makes problems worse; and the more you worry, the less able you are to solve them. But you may not feel like going to someone for advice or sharing them with anyone you know. What do you think people of your age worry about most?

➡ You can do this exercise on your own, or in a small group. Look at this list of things which people commonly worry about. Mark each one out of 10, giving a high mark if you think that young people worry about it a lot, and a low mark if you think young people don't worry about it all that much:

| | |
|---|---|
| money | smoking too much |
| girl/boyfriends | drinking too much |
| loneliness | drug abuse |
| bullying | being mugged or attacked |
| parents | being popular |
| other members of the family | being asked to do something in |
| schoolwork |    public |
| doing badly in exams | being too fat/thin |
| getting a bad school report | being spotty |
| job prospects | the government |
| freedom | war |
| what other people think of you | sex |
| dying | catching sexually transmitted |
| catching a serious illness |    diseases. |

Add any other things which you think should be on this list and aren't.

Now put your list in order, so that the things that you think young people worry about most are at the top. Compare your list with other people's. How similar are they?

In order to see how accurate your views are, you'd have to do a survey. Ask, say, ten other people what they worry about most.

If your parents had to write down the ten things they worried about most, what do you think they'd put? Ask them! What about when your parents were your age? Would they have worried about different things from you? Why do you think this is?
Think about how things are different now. What do we have now that your parents didn't have? Think of ten things — they can be good or bad things. Do your parents think it's easier or more difficult being young now than when they were young?

## Advice columns

Almost every magazine for teenage girls — and for women too — has a problem page or advice page. Some newspapers have them too.

Why would some people rather seek advice from a magazine or newspaper than from people they know?
Would you ever write to an advice column if you had a problem?
What do you think of the advice that is given?

Look at the advice page of a teenage magazine. Can the problems be divided up into those which are practical, and those which are more worrying? In how many cases does the advice given solve the problems? Would you have advised something different?

This is the advice page of a magazine. Some of the questions have been answered. Some are left blank. If you were writing the column, what would you say to the writers?

I'm naturally quiet and I like being alone, but it worries my parents. They keep trying to make me more outgoing. They want me to mix with people at school more, but I don't want to, mainly because they don't like me and call me a snob and a creep behind my back just because I enjoy work and lessons and was too shy to speak to them when I first started school. I don't care, really, because I see them as shallow, thoughtless people with no regard for other people's feelings.
I'm happy the way things are. Why can't my parents see that?
• Are you perfectly sure you're being honest with yourself? Very often, we like people simply because they like us. Similarly, we can take a hearty dislike to people who don't like us!
You got off on the wrong foot with the people at school, something that can so easily happen to people who are shy. Perhaps it is natural on your part to brand them all as not worth knowing. Natural – but a bit negative. If some of this seems to make a bit of sense, then it's not too late to sort things out. Talk to a teacher at school who can help you fit in better.
If you're convinced that you do prefer to be on your own, that friends don't matter, then talk to your parents. Everybody's different – and entitled to be so.
But do think hard. Because it would be awfully easy for you to fool yourself too . . .

I had been going out with Phil for quite some time. But the last time I saw him he was going out with another girl. He said he still loves me but he wants to go out with someone else. I burst into tears. When I got home I tried to kill myself but my friend stopped me. I cry all the time and I know I won't get over it. Please help me before I do kill myself.
Name and address withheld
• It's awful when you are told something like that. Of course you feel shattered, tearful – suicidal even. But you'll get over it; everyone does. One morning you wake up and you're not thinking about it. You know you're on the way back to ordinary life again. But you won't get over it for a long time if you insist that you can't. It's partly an attitude of mind. Do things you enjoy, acquire new skills, and on no account consider suicide – it won't get you anywhere and will upset everyone else.

A group of girls in our class have started picking arguments with us. They say we're childish and immature because we don't talk about boys very much. That's all they ever talk about, you see. They think they're really popular and so experienced but none of them has a steady boyfriend, whereas some of us do.

I do not get on with anyone in my family and I just want to leave home. The problem is I am only 14 and I don't know who to turn to. Could I go to a home or something?

All my friends are allowed out until ten o'clock most nights but while they're out enjoying themselves I'm stuck indoors. I've tried talking things over with my parents, telling them I'm the odd one out but they just don't listen.
My boyfriend's fed up because I'm never allowed out at nights – or if I am, I have to be back so early we can't go anywhere. I'm 14.

Our friend is a compulsive liar. She cons presents out of people at school by telling them she has bought them something really nice. Her friends are disappearing due to her lies. She is becoming two-faced and cannot be trusted. We are very worried about her and can't understand why she is doing this.
Worried ex-friends

Can you divide the problems up into categories? What are most problems about? It's more common for girls to write than boys. Is this because boys don't have problems? If they do have problems, where can they go? Do you think girls tend to discuss their problems more with their friends than boys do?

# Deciding what to do

**?** Fred, Sid, Sophie, and Claire will each have a different approach to making decisions. Which of these approaches would be most likely to fit each person?

1 Looking at all the possible choices, weighing up the advantages and disadvantages of each one, before making a final choice. Gathering any information needed.
3 Not really making a decision at all; just drifting into situations.
3 Panicking.
4 Accepting what someone else says should be done without question.

► Perhaps Sophie is right up to a point. We can't always decide to do exactly as we want. Think of some decisions which you are free to make now, and some which you think you have no control over.
Make a list of them.
Do you think that some time in the future you'll be able to decide more for yourself?
What things will you be able to decide in the future that you can't now? Why?
What will bring about the change?
Have a look at other people's lists of things which they think they can't change now. Do you agree with them?
Do you think they've got more control than they think they have?
What do they think of your list?

## Day-to-day decisions

### Arnold's decisions

1 The alarm goes. Should he skip breakfast and annoy his mother for the sake of an extra sleep? How can he get to bed earlier at night?
2 What should he wear?
3 Will it rain? Should he cycle or take the bus?
4 On the way to school he sees an old lady trip and fall. Should he go and help, even though he'll be late?
5 He hasn't really done the work for this lesson. Should he cheat and get someone to help him?
6 He ought to talk to his teacher about next year's subjects. Should he do that today, or go to football practice?
7 On the way home he passes an advertisement for a part-time job. Should he go and find out about it?
8 How much homework should he do before he goes to see his friend Bob?

**?** How many decisions did Arnold have to make?
What sort were they — important, not important, short-term or long-term? Make a table of them.
Imagine you are Arnold. What would you decide to do in each case?
How would you make each decision? Would you consider the effects of the decision? Would you weigh up any information?

**?** How many decisions have you made today?
What sort were they?
How did you decide?
Do they have long- or short-term effects?
Do you think people's personalities affect the way they make decisions?

## Different people's reactions

Darrell is strong, aggressive, and likes to think he's tough.
Tony is very lively and impulsive; he doesn't always think before he acts.
Lizzie is very mild and doesn't like to offend anyone.
Cheryl is thoughtful and always likes to cover all the possibilities before she does anything.
Kenny is shy and nervous.

**?** What decisions do you think Darrell, Tony, Lizzie, Cheryl, and Kenny would make in the following situations?
1 Being late for school.
2 Seeing someone knocked off his or her motorbike.
3 Considering what to do after being wrongly accused of stealing something at school.
4 Being offered a part-time job.
5 Wondering whether to skip school one day.
Do other people agree with what you've said?

**?** What are the choices open in these situations?
1 The bus is late, and you're going to miss an important appointment for an interview. Here are some options:
  a Think 'It's fate; I never wanted to go anyway', and go home.
  b Wait and wait for the next bus and hope you can explain when you get there.
  c Try to hitch.
  d Phone the place you're supposed to be at and explain.

Are there other options you can think of which aren't mentioned? What are they?
What do you think *you* would do?
Is what you would do necessarily the best decision?
What do you think Darrell, Tony, Cheryl, Lizzie, and Kenny would do?

2 You've been to a party. The people who brought you in their car have had too much to drink. You don't think you should go with them, but there aren't any buses.

What are the choices? Think of as many as possible.
What do you think you would be most likely to do?
What about Darrell, Tony, Cheryl, Lizzie, and Kenny?

3 You feel you're being bullied at school.
  How many different ways can you think of to cope with it?

# Making long-term decisions

You may already be considering decisions which will affect your life for some time to come: decisions such as what subjects to take, what to do after leaving school, what to do if you can't get a job.

> But I don't know what I want to do, I don't know which subjects are best. And it's all a long way away. How will I know what the right decision to make is?

**?** How can you find out more?
Who are the people to talk to at your school about career and subject choices?
Have you met the Careers Officer?
Have you got a careers library?
What sort of jobs are available in your area?
What could you do if you can't get a job?
What further education courses are there?

## Developing a strategy

1 Rona is interested in looking after children. She's doing appropriate CSEs at school. She doesn't know whether she's good enough to follow a college course, or what courses are available. People tell her that the courses are very difficult to get on. Perhaps she'd be better with some experience? Suddenly, the people that she baby-sits for announce that they are going to Australia for a year in September. They'd like Rona to go with them as a mother's help. They would pay her expenses and give her a small allowance. She would be treated like one of the family, and may be asked to stay with them after they return.

2 Harry doesn't want to stay at school. He knows he'd be happier at work. For some time he's been building up his own small business at weekends, providing kindling and firewood for local houses. It's hard work, but he's strong. He's making quite good money. He thinks the work would provide a living if he did it full time, but there would always be the risks attached to working for himself. A friend of his who works for a haulage firm says that the firm is looking for a lad to train up as mate and delivery boy, with eventual training in HGV work. The pay isn't good, but the firm is doing well and a job with them would probably be secure.

**?** 1 What information do you think Rona and Harry need?
2 Where would they find it?
3 Who could help them with advice?
4 Who might they go and talk to about their decisions?
5 What advantages and disadvantages do they have to consider?
6 What might happen to them in each case?
7 Finish these sentences for them:
If Rona goes to Australia, she . . .
If Harry goes on working for himself, he . . .
8 Could you predict what their lives might be like in five or ten years' time?
9 Do you think their ambitions will have changed?

# Forming values and judgements

Talking about what people think is important in their lives brings us to the question of how we form our values, and how we make judgements. If someone said to you 'Tell me what your values are', you'd probably find it hard to answer. So we'll start by looking at the things which you regard as important.

▶ List ten things you like doing — playing football? going to parties? listening to music? Make a table like this one to show how long you've been doing them, who you like doing them with, and where you like to do them.

| ACTIVITY | HOW LONG? | WHO WITH? | WHERE? |
|---|---|---|---|
|  |  |  |  |

Does anything surprise you about the list?
Now do the same sort of table, but this time, fill it in with the things that you liked doing two years ago.
How has the list changed?
Complete these sentences:
  I was surprised to see that . . .
  From doing this exercise I have learnt that . . .

Who are the most important people to you now? Beside their names, write down their relationship to you, and how long you have known them.
What would you have put two years ago?
Is the list different?
Can you say how it has changed? For example, this is what Sherry found when she did this exercise:

When I was twelve, the most important people to me were my parents and one good friend. Now I see that I place more importance on my group of friends. I talk to them more than I do to my parents. I have also got very friendly with my best friend's mum.

Some values change, as you can see from the exercise comparing what you like doing now with what you liked doing two years ago.

❓ Can you say if the values of your older brother, sister, or friends are different from yours?
If they are, can you say how?

What about your parents? What do they think is important?
Are their values different from yours?
How and why?